"If you're looking for one book to help you underst[a], this is the best out there. The author is definitely the guru on grief; he truly gets it. I found this after losing my husband, and I felt like it helped save me!"

"It's so thoughtful, compassionate, and empathetic to the reader. It's like a warm hug on my heart."

"Your words have helped me deal with the loss of my husband, and I sincerely thank you. I've since bought several other books of yours and they, too, are of great help through this wilderness."

"This book has been more beneficial to me than almost anything. I am so thankful my therapist recommended it."

"I have been a certified grief counselor in Acclaim Hospice since it began. I have used your book and journal in every support group, companioning hundreds of people on their unique journey. What an honor!"

"I cannot begin to tell you how this book helped me as I walked through the pain, confusion, and 'insanity' back to stability. Thank you for helping give words to what I could not as well as hope for what I could not yet see."

"I love the author's sound concepts and always-compassionate tone. I am so glad I found this book."

"I lost my husband last November. I didn't know it would hurt so bad. I just wanted to write and say a heartfelt thank you for your book. It is beautiful."

"After almost four years on the grief path, this is by far the best book I've read to date. I wish I had it at the start of my journey. I recommend Understanding Your Grief to everyone I know."

"I lost my dearly loved lady about five weeks ago. I just finished your book, and I cannot tell you how helpful it has been for me."

"The wilderness you talk about is exactly where I am. Your book is wonderful, and it is helping me find my way. I pray the book and journal will help both me and my son as we journey through this wilderness and find our way to joyful living again."

"Throughout the support group, discussing and sharing each touchstone in detail was so beneficial, which got everyone, and I mean everyone, to open up and talk about their loss."

"Of all the books I've read since my son was killed (and there are plenty), this one would be at the top of the list. It validates and fortifies the bereaved, and it shows the way to integrate grief toward a new life of hope as our loved ones would want us to live."

"I must say this is a special book. I've been feeling lost, and people are unable to see what I'm going through or try to tell me what I should be doing. And then there is this book, which is like a person reaching out and saying, 'I understand.'"

"I bought this book for my brother-in-law after his wife passed. He has thanked me every time he sees me and shows me excerpts that have helped him understand and cope with his loss."

"After searching for over a year for a book to soothe my grieving heart after the death of my husband...this book is it."

"Best book ever if you are going through a loss. With understanding comes comfort. It also helped with talking about grief, making it easier to reach out to others. Highly recommend."

"I write to you with such gratitude. You truly cover every aspect and context of grief that we human beings can possibly experience. Your resources pulled me out of one of the greatest sorrows since the death of my father. The grief journal, in particular, gave me a place to be asked hard questions— questions I didn't realize needed to be answered."

UNDERSTANDING YOUR

[SECOND EDITION]

ALSO BY ALAN WOLFELT

The Understanding Your Grief Journal:
Exploring the Ten Essential Touchstones

Companioning the Bereaved:
A Soulful Guide for Caregivers

Healing Your Grieving Heart:
100 Practical Ideas

Grief One Day at a Time:
365 Meditations to Help You Heal After Loss

Healing a Parent's Grieving Heart:
100 Practical Ideas After Your Child Dies

The Journey Through Grief:
Reflections On Healing

Loving from the Outside In,
Mourning from the Inside Out

UNDERSTANDING YOUR

Grief

TEN ESSENTIAL TOUCHSTONES
FOR FINDING HOPE AND
HEALING YOUR HEART

[SECOND EDITION]

ALAN D. WOLFELT, PH.D.

Companion
PRESS

Fort Collins, Colorado
An imprint of the Center for Loss and Life Transition

Companion
PRESS

Companion Press is dedicated to the education and support
of both the bereaved and bereavement caregivers. We believe that those
who companion the bereaved by walking with them as they journey in
grief have a wondrous opportunity: to help others embrace and
grow through grief—and to lead fuller, more deeply-lived lives
themselves because of this important ministry.

For a complete catalog and ordering information, write or call:

Companion Press
The Center for Loss and Life Transition
3735 Broken Bow Road
Fort Collins, CO 80526
(970) 226-6050
www.centerforloss.com

First edition, ISBN 978-1-879651-35-7 © 2004 by Alan D. Wolfelt, Ph.D.

Second edition, ISBN 978-1-61722-307-5 © 2021 by Alan D. Wolfelt, Ph.D.

Companion Press is an imprint of the
Center for Loss and Life Transition
3735 Broken Bow Road
Fort Collins, Colorado 80526

Printed in the United States of America

30 29 28 27 26 25 24   5 4

ISBN: 978-1-61722-307-5

*To the thousands of journeyers who have invited me
to walk with them through the wilderness of their grief.*

What you have taught me I teach to others.

Thank you for entrusting me with your stories of love and loss.

The *Understanding Your Grief* Series

SECOND EDITION

This book is designed to be used along with
The Understanding Your Grief Journal, Second Edition,
also by Dr. Alan Wolfelt. There is also a support group faciliator
guide available entitled *The Understanding Your Grief
Support Group Guide, Second Edition*.

There is also a daily reader version titled
365 Days of Understanding Your Grief. This text serves
as ideal supplemental reading for the griever.

Contents

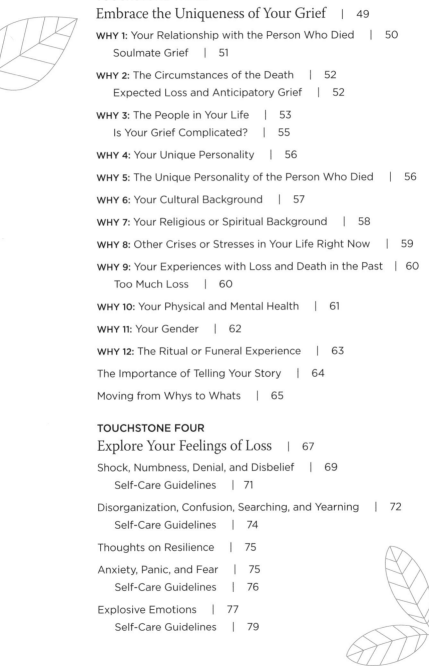

Foreword

Some call grief a journey. I call it a quest. Grief stuns us, and we quickly surrender to isolation, disbelief, and uncertainty. From that moment on, we're on a search for help to survive and reassurance we're not crazy.

> "*To know the road ahead, ask those coming back.*"
> Chinese proverb

I can personally bear witness to grief's life-changing nature. Challenged by the unexpected suicide death of our son, Chad, in 1993, my husband and I felt abandoned and scared, looking for answers and the courage and strength to go on. Chad's fiancée died by suicide ten weeks later.

Early in our quest, we met Dr. Alan Wolfelt at the urging of a local funeral director. I'll never forget the day we attended one of his conferences in a nearby town. We thought, "If only we could have a moment of his time to share our story and get some guidance." Not only did he agree to meet with us alone, but he also graciously took time to listen, encourage, and validate our grieving needs. He also offered us the first version of this book for ongoing guidance. Soon after, we became students and graduates of his Center for Loss, and since then we have shared his teachings with countless others.

We use *Understanding Your Grief* as a resource and guide for our grief/education support groups, which we've facilitated since 1996.

This book and the companion journal are the framework we use to encourage participants. What we appreciate is that *Understanding Your Grief* doesn't tell you what to think or feel. Instead, it leads you gently through the principles and feelings of grief and helps you become acquainted with your own mysteries.

Our participants respond to this book with sincere gratitude. It provides exactly the information they need. Writing out their thoughts in the journal (or even just pondering those thoughts) further helps them make peace with their healing quest.

Dr. Wolfelt's teachings evolve from his own loss experiences as well as the expressions of others, deep in grief, speaking from their heart. He also continues to mentor dedicated caregivers searching for ways to better companion grieving people. *Understanding Your Grief* wraps all this wisdom into one volume. For us personally, no resource has touched us more or was better able to soothe the battling emotions that threatened to pull us over the edge. The valuable updates in this second edition demonstrate his ongoing commitment to support grieving people.

If you are on a quest to understand your own grief, this book is for you. It's not the kind of book you read once then put on your shelf as a trophy. Instead, it's a compass, a traveler's guide, and a beacon for the meandering days of grief ahead. It's a book you open multiple times to verify first inklings and confirm, "Yes, this is normal. This is my grief." It speaks to you in compassionate, simple terms that authenticate your thoughts, feelings, and uncertainties. And it helps you mourn actively and openly, which will carry you forward.

When you are wounded by grief, trust the words of Dr. Wolfelt. They will help you find the best path for you. It is the path to hope and healing.

Nan Zastrow
Founder, Wings—A Grief Education Ministry
Wausau, Wisconsin
wingsgrief.org

Preface

The death of those precious to us changes our lives forever. I discovered this reality as a boy, when several of my family members and friends died. To be bereaved means to be torn apart and have special needs. While I didn't know the word, I instinctively felt bereaved, yet I was dismayed that no one around me talked about the deaths. What's more, no one continued to check in with me about my thoughts and feelings or offer me ongoing compassion and comfort. It was as if the deaths never happened, yet inside me I was experiencing deep pain and many confusing new thoughts and feelings.

Even a child can see that our culture doesn't do grief well. In fact, it was then that I decided that when I grew up, I would try to be a force for change and an advocate for grieving people. I would make it my life's work to evolve our culture's understanding of grief and how to support one another after a loss.

And so it came to be that I found my calling at a young age. I went on to become a thanatologist (a fancy word for grief counselor) and death educator, and I founded the Center for Loss and Life Transition. It was then—over thirty years ago now—that I wrote the first iteration of this book, called *Understanding Grief*. I was still relatively new to my vocation, but what I deeply understood was that grief was a normal, necessary part of human life. And I wanted to put a book out into the world that would help as many people as possible when they—as we all do—inevitably come to grief.

In 2004, I published an updated version of the book, now titled *Understanding Your Grief* (because while all grief experiences have much in common, your grief is always unique). I'm so grateful to report that *Understanding Your Grief* went on to reach hundreds of thousands of grievers and, together with its companion journal, continues to be used as the resources for many grief support groups.

Last year I decided it was again time for an update. Since 2004, I'd done a great deal more learning, teaching, and writing, and I had some new thoughts to share. This second edition of *Understanding Your Grief* contains a number of concise additions and clarity edits. It also has a fresh, updated look. While the book's basic principles, touchstones, and structure remain the same, you'll find new tidbits on topics such as resilience, vulnerability, soulmate grief, grief overload, complicated grief, mindfulness, the power of ritual, and others. In general, I hope you'll also enjoy a smoother reading experience.

Concurrently, I've updated *The Understanding Your Grief Journal* and *The Understanding Your Grief Support Group Guide*, too. Please be sure to use the second editions of these resources as well so that page-number and topic references align.

I'm also gratified to report that since the time I was a grieving child, and especially during the last two decades since the publication of the first *Understanding Your Grief*, our culture has gotten a bit better at acknowledging and supporting grief. While we still have a ways to go, I've seen progress. We're awakening to mental health issues and the idea of holistic wellness. We're beginning to leave behind dated, harmful constructs about what it means to "be strong." We're developing more emotional intelligence and are more apt to talk openly about losses and the difficult feelings that naturally go hand-in-hand with them. We're appreciating, more and more, the importance of good self-care physically, cognitively, emotionally, socially, and spiritually.

As this second edition of *Understanding Your Grief* finds its way into grievers' hands over the future years, my fervent hope is that we'll continue to get even better at loving and taking care of ourselves and one another, especially when we are torn apart by loss. In addition to helping you, the individual reader, I believe that excellent, universal grief awareness and support have the power to change the world. Why? Because if we can build genuine, deep empathy into every interaction in human life—and I know it's there, because love is there—we can find our way past every deep-seated problem, from violence and poverty to climate change and more.

As I write to you on America's one-year anniversary of the start of the COVID-19 pandemic—a tragedy that has enhanced our cultural understanding of loss and the need for grief support—I have never been more hopeful about the future or more grateful for this life.

I hope we meet one day.

Alan D. Wolfelt

Introduction

You've probably picked up this book because someone you love has died. You're no doubt hurting and in search of understanding, compassion, and solace. My sincere hope is that you will find all of these in the following pages. I'm so glad you're here.

> "Where you used to be, there is a hole in the world, which I find myself walking around in the daytime, and falling in at night. I miss you like hell."
>
> Edna St. Vincent Millay

Grief is as old as humankind, yet every time a unique human being loses someone they love or suffers any significant loss, it is a freshly painful, singular experience. I offer you my deepest and most genuine condolences.

As a grief counselor of more than forty years, I understand that your grief is breathtakingly real and present—and naturally overwhelming. Yet by picking up this book when you're hurting, you're taking one small but oh-so-important step toward integrating this loss into your life. Actively engaging with your grief in this way may not only help you feel a bit of comfort in the moment, it's a wise course in the longer term because **grief responds to attention and expression**. I often say that **grief waits on welcome, not on time**. We'll be talking a lot more about that soon.

So here's a good rule of thumb as you read this book and for the days ahead: Whenever you're feeling your grief, I would suggest you take a few seconds or minutes to tend to it in some way. I say this because your grief will keep trying to get your attention until you give it the attention it deserves.

In these moments, how you give your grief attention is up to you. Sit with your grief and cry. Or talk to a friend about it. Or jot down some thoughts in a notebook. Or text another person grieving the same loss. Or pick up this book and read a page or two.

SURVIVING THE EARLY DAYS

If your loss was recent, you may find that you're not yet ready to engage with the contents of this book. Feelings of shock and numbness naturally dominate early grief, as does a diminished ability to concentrate. These normal responses may make it difficult, if not impossible, to read through the following touchstones and feel like you're being helped by the experience.

> *"There's a fine edge to new grief. It severs nerves, disconnects reality—there's a mercy in a sharp blade. Only with time, as the edge wears, does the real ache begin."*
>
> Christopher Moore

So if you were given this book by a well-intentioned friend or purchased it yourself shortly after a death—only to find that you can't focus on it or it doesn't speak to your immediate needs—I encourage you to set it aside for the time being.

Instead, concentrate on doing whatever you need to do to survive, one day at a time. Breathe in and breathe out. Turn to your friends and family members. Comfort yourself however you can. Reach out to a counselor if you're finding it unbearable to make it through each day.

Later on, when the shock and psychic numbness start to wear off and you're regaining the capacity to focus, try picking up this book and the companion journal again. I believe they can help you, but it's a matter of timing. Go at your own pace, and come back whenever you're ready.

Your grief needs you right now. And as difficult as it is, you need your grief—because it is now an essential part of your life and who you are.

Understanding as Surrendering

The title of this book is *Understanding Your Grief*. Indeed, one of the most important things I hope I do as a caregiver to grieving people is offer information that helps you understand and integrate loss into your life. What's more, I strive to help you discern and avoid some of the unnecessary pain sometimes caused by well-intentioned but misinformed friends, family members, and even some professional counselors. They sometimes perpetuate grief misconceptions, proffer misguided advice, and impose unrealistic and inappropriate expectations on those who are mourning. Though they don't do this knowingly, they can in effect pull you off the path toward healing.

> *"The moment of surrender is not when life is over, it's when it begins."*
>
> Marianne Williamson

But there's also a paradox built into the concept of "understanding" grief. Yes, when the timing seems right and mourners are ready to learn from those who've walked the path of loss before them, I try my best to provide information and education that affirms what they are experiencing and helps them understand it. However, sometimes it's the very need to totally understand the experience of grief that can get you in trouble. Because it turns out that **the mysteries of life and death can't be fully explained but must instead be pondered**.

Sometimes we simply cannot understand the death of someone we love so deeply. We can't understand it now, and we will not understand it ever. I certainly couldn't understand why the doctors couldn't cure my dad's melanoma. "It's only skin cancer," I thought. I didn't understand—I protested!

I've learned that sometimes it is in staying open to the mystery and recognizing that we *don't* understand and *can't* control everything in life that understanding eventually unfolds. In fact, perhaps it is "standing under" the mysterious experience of death that provides us with a unique perspective: We are not above or bigger than death. Maybe only after exhausting the search for trying to understand why someone we love had to die can we discover a newly defined "why" for our own life.

So instead of doggedly pursuing understanding, I invite you to first befriend the concept of surrender. In my experience, **understanding begins to dawn only after we surrender**: surrender our need to compare our grief (it's not a competition); surrender our self-critical judgments (we need to be self-compassionate); and surrender our need to completely understand all the secrets of life and death (we never will). In other words, the grief that pervades our souls has its own mysterious plan, which should not be compromised by our need for comparison, judgment, or even complete understanding.

UNDERSTANDING ALL YOUR GRIEFS

From the moment we are born, life is a series of transitions and losses. Along the way, whenever we are separated from anyone or anything important to us, we experience important grief. And so divorce, illness, estrangement, pet loss, traumatic events, relocation, financial loss, job loss, and other common types of loss may break our hearts, too. Even in happier transition circumstances—such as graduations, weddings, and retirements—any time we gain something new, we give something else up.

This book is about the grief that follows death loss. However, if you are also feeling the equally valid grief of non-death losses, you will find that parts of this book may have some application to those circumstances as well. While each type of loss has its own unique features, there are also commonalities. So no matter the particulars of the losses you have experienced in your life, I welcome you to this conversation.

Yet also please note that surrender is not the same as resignation. I am absolutely not asking you to resign yourself to a future of misery. Actually, surrendering to the unknowable mystery is a courageous choice, an act of faith, a trust in God or a higher power, and in ourselves. We can only hold this mystery in our hearts and surround ourselves with love.

EXPRESS YOURSELF:
Go to *The Understanding Your Grief Journal* on p. 10.

The Ten Touchstones

In this book, I will describe ten "touchstones" that are essential physical, cognitive, emotional, social, and spiritual signs for mourners to seek out on their journey through grief:

TOUCHSTONE ONE	Open to the presence of your loss
TOUCHSTONE TWO	Dispel a dozen misconceptions about grief
TOUCHSTONE THREE	Embrace the uniqueness of your grief
TOUCHSTONE FOUR	Explore your feelings of loss
TOUCHSTONE FIVE	Understand the six needs of mourning
TOUCHSTONE SIX	Recognize you are not crazy
TOUCHSTONE SEVEN	Nurture yourself
TOUCHSTONE EIGHT	Reach out for help
TOUCHSTONE NINE	Seek reconciliation, not resolution
TOUCHSTONE TEN	Appreciate your transformation

Think of your grief as a wilderness—a vast, mountainous, inhospitable forest. You are in the wilderness now. You are in the midst of unfamiliar and often brutal surroundings. You are cold and tired. Yet you must journey through this wilderness. To find your way out, you must become acquainted with its terrain and learn to follow the sometimes hard-to-find trail that leads to healing.

In this wilderness of your grief, **the touchstones are your trail**

markers. They are the signs that let you know you are on the right path. When you learn to identify and rely on the touchstones, you will not get lost in your journey, even though the trail will often be arduous and you may at times feel hopeless.

And even when you've become a master journeyer and you know well the terrain of your grief, you will probably sometimes feel like you're backtracking, getting lost, or being ravaged by the forces around you. This, too, is the nature of grief. Complete mastery (like complete understanding) of a wilderness is simply not possible. Just as we can't control the winds and the storms and the beasts in nature, we can never have total dominion over our grief.

But if you actively engage with your grief, if you become an intrepid traveler on your journey, if you strive to follow these ten touchstones, I believe you can and will find your way out of the wilderness of your grief, and you will learn to make the most of the rest of your precious days here on earth.

EXPRESS YOURSELF:
Go to *The Understanding Your Grief Journal* on p. 11.

Finding Hope

Hope is an equally important foundation in this book.

What is hope? **Hope is an expectation of a good that is yet to be**. It's an expression of the present alive with a sense of the possible. It's a future-looking expectation felt in the present moment.

In grief, hope is a belief that healing can and will unfold, and that despite the loss, there will surely be many meaningful, engaging, fun, happy, and even joyful times to come. In honoring the ten touchstones, you are making an effort to find hope for your continued life. Through deliberate mourning, you yourself can be the purveyor of your hope. You cultivate hope in yourself by actively engaging with and expressing your grief as well as regularly setting and affirming your intention to heal.

When you feel hopeless, which you probably will now and then, you can also reach out to others for hope. In other words, you can borrow hope by spending time in the company of people who support your need to mourn yet at the same time give you hope for healing. People who are empathetic, nonjudgmental, good listeners and who model positive, optimistic ways of being in the world will be your best grief companions. They will resupply you with hope when your stores are running low. They will help you build divine momentum toward your eventual exodus from the wilderness of your grief.

EXPRESS YOURSELF:
Go to *The Understanding Your Grief Journal* on p. 12.

DIVINE MOMENTUM

Now and then in this book you'll hear me talk about "divine momentum" in the grief journey. This is the experience of being propelled toward healing by doing what is helpful and necessary.

Sometimes after you've actively worked on one of the six needs of mourning (see page 93), you may notice that you feel a bubble of hope or buoyed by a sense of movement toward reconciliation. You'll realize that you're authentically befriending and expressing your grief, and, slowly and over time, healing. These moments of awareness are indicators of divine momentum.

Divine momentum is the opposite of being stuck. When you're feeling stuck in your grief journey—which will happen, too, sometimes—you can remember to turn to those mourning activities and practices that restart your divine momentum.

Healing Your Heart

I also insisted that the word "heart" be included in the title of this book. Why? Because my years of learning from my own losses as well as the losses of the thousands of people who have trusted me to walk alongside them in grief have taught me that an open heart that is grieving is a "well of reception;" it is moved entirely by what it has perceived. Authentic mourning is an opportunity to embrace that open heart in ways that allow for and encourage healing.

Perhaps the most central truth I have learned over the years is that **healing in grief is heart-based, not head-based**. Modern therapies sometimes separate the mind from the heart; it's as if we should somehow be able to rationally think through our grief. I *heart*ily disagree! Carl Jung taught us years ago that every psychological struggle is ultimately a matter of spirituality. The contents of this book encourage you to think, yes, but more importantly, to feel with your heart and your soul.

> *"There are pains that cannot be contained in the mind—only in the heart."*
>
> Stephen Levine

Did you know that the word "courage" comes from the Old French word for heart (*coeur*)? Your courage grows for those things in life that impact you deeply. The death of someone you treasure opens, or engages, your heart. Now you must take your heart, which has been engaged, and muster the courage to encounter the ten essential touchstones. Courage can also be defined as the ability to do what one believes is right, despite the fact that others may strongly and persuasively disagree. If this book helps you authentically mourn, some may try to shame you. Nevertheless, you must go forth with courage.

This book, directed from my heart to yours, is an invitation to go to that spiritual place inside yourself and, transcending our mourning-avoidant society and even your own personal inhibitions about grief, enter deeply into the journey. In many ways the path of the heart is an individual exploration into the wilderness, along unmarked and unlit paths. I hope this book will shine some light along your path.

EXPRESS YOURSELF:
Go to *The Understanding Your Grief Journal* on p. 13.

A Word About Faith and Spirituality

Readers new to my work may wonder if this is a religious book, a nonreligious book, or something in between.

What I believe is that grief is first and foremost a spiritual journey because it forces us to examine our most fundamental beliefs and feelings about why we are here and what life means. To me, spirituality means engaging with these big questions and the deepest, most meaningful stirrings of your heart in whatever ways you choose.

While I was raised in the Methodist church, I invite all spiritual traditions, understandings, and practices to this discussion. You may sometimes hear me use the words or concepts of "God," "faith," or "soul," for example. Take or leave them as you will, and feel free to substitute your own understanding.

Whether you are deeply religious, agnostic, or atheist, you grieve and must express your grief. Pondering the meaning of life and love and the possibilities of the mysteries we do not and cannot fully understand is an essential part of your journey. Regularly spending time on spiritual practices—whatever that means to you—will help you embrace your grief and come out of the dark and into the light. I'll be talking more about that in the touchstones ahead.

EXPRESS YOURSELF:
Go to *The Understanding Your Grief Journal* on p. 14.

Owning and Honoring Your Journey

I have attempted to convey in the following pages an active empathy, encouraging you to **own your rightful role as expert of your own grief experience**. You see, I have discovered a touchstone in my own personal walks into grief and in my "companioning" of fellow human beings: I can only help people when I encourage them to teach me about their unique journeys into grief.

You may consider this helping attitude strange. After all, as a professional grief counselor, am I not supposed to "treat" the person who has come to me for help? No, not really. My experience has made me aware that thinking a trained counselor like myself should have all the answers for grieving people only complicates their experience. Some traditional grief therapies tend to be controlling. The counselor is supposed to be "in charge" and to know what is best for the person in grief. However, I believe this treatment-oriented, more prescriptive approach can be harmful as opposed to helpful.

Instead, if I encourage you to be my teacher, I not only become more helpful to you, but I am enriched and changed in meaningful ways in my own life. Likewise, if you as mourner conceive of yourself as the teacher or expert of your own grief—as the master of the journey that is your grief—you will feel empowered to own what you are feeling and not feel shamed or deterred by the sometimes judgmental responses of others. You will also learn to seek out the support of those who naturally adopt a companioning attitude toward you and avoid those who don't.

Depending on the nature of your loss, you may also feel supported in your unique journey by reading or keeping at hand one of my books on specialized types of loss, ranging from the death of a spouse, child, or parent to traumatic loss, stillbirth, suicide loss, and many more. I have also written books for the grieving children and teenagers in your life. You'll find a complete list of my books for mourners at the end of this book in the Further Reading appendix on page 208.

EXPRESS YOURSELF:
Go to *The Understanding Your Grief Journal* on p. 15.

COMPANIONING VERSUS TREATING

To help you feel empowered to be in charge of your own grief, please allow me to share with you a little about my grief counseling philosophy, which I call "companioning."

The word "treat" comes from the Latin root word *tractare*, which means "to drag." If we combine that with the word "patient," we can really get in trouble. "Patient" means "passive long-term sufferer." So if as a grief counselor I treat patients, I drag passive long-term sufferers.

On the other hand, the word "companion," when broken down into its original Latin roots means "messmate": *com* for "with" and *pan* for "bread." Someone you would share a meal with, a friend, an equal. I have taken liberties with the noun "companion" and made it into the verb "companioning" because it so well captures the type of counseling relationship I support and advocate.

More specifically, grief counselors who embrace the companioning model understand that:

- Companioning is about being present to another person's pain; it is not about taking away the pain.

- Companioning is about going to the wilderness of the soul with another human being; it is not about thinking you are responsible for finding the way out.

- Companioning is about honoring the spirit; it is not about focusing on the intellect.

- Companioning is about listening with the heart; it is not about analyzing with the head.

- Companioning is about bearing witness to the struggles of others; it is not about judging or directing these struggles.

- Companioning is about walking alongside; it is not about leading.

(Continued on next page.)

- Companioning is about discovering the gifts of sacred silence; it is not about filling up every moment with words.

- Companioning is about being still; it is not about frantic movement forward.

- Companioning is about respecting disorder and confusion; it is not about imposing order and logic.

- Companioning is about learning from others; it is not about teaching them.

- Companioning is about compassionate curiosity; it is not about expertise.

I always invite—and sometimes even challenge—counselors who come to my trainings at the Center for Loss in Fort Collins, Colorado, to adopt a companioning, teach-me attitude with people in grief. When we think of ourselves as grief companions, we counselors are less likely to make inappropriate interpretations or judgments of the mourner's experiences. This approach helps ensure that when a person in grief expresses thoughts, feelings, or attitudes, we consciously avoid making evaluative reactions like, "That's right or wrong," "That shouldn't be," or worse yet, "That's pathological." Instead, all responses are valid, and everything belongs.

How to Use This Book

My purpose in the pages that follow is to provide an opportunity for you to learn about your own unique journey into the wilderness that is grief. As you have without doubt already discovered, grief is an intensely personal experience. No two people will ever grieve and mourn in the same way, even when they are mourning the death of the same person. Your own grief is unlike anyone else's, even though you will find that you often have experiences in common with others in grief. I hope you discover this book to be a safe place to embrace what you uniquely think and feel without fear of being judged.

One of the concerns I have about many grief books is that they try to tell you, the reader, what to think and feel. This book, however, allows and encourages you to explore how you think and feel right now. It is descriptive rather than prescriptive. While it does describe ten essential touchstones, you will find that each of these touchstones will be "lived" and experienced in different ways by different people. **The key is not to fit your experience to the touchstones but instead to fit the touchstones to your experience.**

The companion journal to this book (*The Understanding Your Grief Journal—Second Edition*) provides you a dedicated place to write out your thoughts and feelings about the content of this book as you read it. Neither this book nor the journal attempt to prescribe how you should feel, because integrating a death into your life demands that you embrace your own unique responses, thoughts, and feelings.

So, I invite you to read this book with an eye to gleaning from it only what makes sense to you and your unique journey. I also encourage you to complete the companion journal. Journaling in grief is a powerful method for helping yourself heal. A journal allows you to express your innermost thoughts and feelings about grief outside of yourself even as you keep them private. If you don't have access to the companion journal, you may simply want to use a spiral notebook and make notes to yourself as you read this text. Whenever you see the cue "Express Yourself," simply ask yourself how what you've just read applies to your own grief, then write your thoughts and feelings in your notebook.

If you're not a journaler, that's OK, too. Not everyone feels comfortable expressing themselves through the written word. Talking about what you're reading in this book with someone who cares is another effective way to explore the touchstones and do your work of mourning.

EXPRESS YOURSELF:
Go to *The Understanding Your Grief Journal* on p. 16.

In Gratitude

I thank you for taking the time to read and reflect on the words that make up this book. It is people just like you who have been my teachers. I am also grateful to the thousands of people who have participated in my retreat learning experiences about grief and who have embraced the companioning philosophy I hold so dear. Most important, I thank those who have gone before me for teaching me that grief is a birthright of life and that giving and receiving love is the essence of having meaning and purpose in our lives.

If you find this book helpful, I hope you will write to me about your journey and allow me to learn from you as I have from countless others who have been touched by the death of someone loved.

365 DAYS OF UNDERSTANDING YOUR GRIEF

Grief support group leaders who use *Understanding Your Grief* and its companion journal as foundational texts for their groups asked me to write another book to help support group

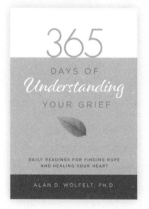

graduates carry their newfound understanding forward. *365 Days of Understanding Your Grief* was the result.

This daily version of *Understanding Your Grief* parses the text into tiny, digestible bits. At the same time, it also expands the content, adding lots of new ideas and guidance. You can read one without the other or both—together or sequentially.

If you think you would feel supported by a brief daily reader, I invite you to add *365 Days of Understanding Your Grief* to your nightstand and spend five minutes with it each morning when you awake.

Open to the
Presence of Your Loss

When someone you love dies, the pain of grief arises naturally, and it is normal.

From my own experiences with loss as well as those of the many grieving people I have companioned over the years, I have learned that the pain of grief is both normal and necessary. We cannot go around the pain that is the wilderness of our grief. Instead, we must journey all through it, sometimes shuffling along the less strenuous side paths, sometimes plowing directly into the dark center.

In opening to the presence of the pain of your loss, in acknowledging the inevitability and appropriateness of the pain, in being willing to gently embrace the pain, you in effect honor the pain. "What?" you may naturally protest, "Honor the pain?"

Yes, as crazy as it may sound, **your pain is the key that opens your heart and ushers you on your way to healing**.

In many ways, although it may seem strange, the purpose of this book is to help you honor your pain. Honoring means recognizing

WHAT IS HEALING IN GRIEF?

Throughout this book we will be talking about the goal of healing your grief, so it's important that we define it up front.

To heal in grief is to become whole again, to integrate your grief into your self and to learn to continue your changed life with fullness and meaning. Experiencing a new and changed "wholeness" requires that you engage in the work of mourning. It doesn't just happen to you; to heal you must actively attend to and express that which has broken you.

Healing is a holistic concept that embraces the physical, cognitive, emotional, social, and spiritual realms. Note that healing is not the same as "curing," which is a medical term that means "remedying" or "correcting." You cannot remedy your grief, but you can reconcile it. You cannot correct your grief, but you can heal it.

the value of and respecting. I believe that we are born with an instinctive understanding of the need to mourn. That is why when we're children we immediately cry, fuss, and get upset when we experience discomfort or loss of any kind. As we grow up, however, our culture teaches us that it is polite to keep such feelings inside us. Consciously or unconsciously, we learn that expressing our natural grief when others are around to see and hear it is often considered immature, out-of-control, unnecessary, and/or socially unacceptable. But it is our culture that is wrong—not our instincts. Simply put, **the capacity to love requires the necessity to mourn**. To honor your grief is not self-destructive or harmful; it is self-sustaining and life-giving!

> "Grief can be the garden of compassion. If you keep your heart open through everything, your pain can become your greatest ally in your life's search for love and wisdom."
>
> Rumi

Along the way, you have also likely been taught that pain, in general, is an indication that something is wrong and that it's your job to find ways to alleviate the pain, if not mask it altogether. You may think of pain and feelings of loss as experiences to avoid, suppress, or deny. Why? Because the role of pain and suffering is misunderstood.

> "We must embrace pain and burn it as fuel for our journey."
>
> Kenji Miyazawa

Often combined with these messages is an unstated but strong belief that "You have a right not to hurt. You deserve to not hurt. So do whatever is necessary to avoid it." Dismiss this trite suggestion, also. If you don't, the unfortunate result may be that you try to medicate away your pain, go around your hurt, or deny any and all feelings of loss.

Naturally, if you avoid your pain, the people around you will not have to be with you as you experience it, either. While this may be more comfortable for them, it would prove to be unhealthy for you. The reality is that many people will try to shield themselves from your pain by trying to protect you from it. Try your best not let anyone do this to you.

Over time you will learn that the pain of your grief will keep trying to get your attention until you have the courage to gently, and in small doses, open to its presence. You will also learn that the alternative—denying or suppressing your pain—is in fact more harmful in the long run. I have learned that the pain that surrounds the *closed* heart of grief is the pain of living against yourself, the pain of denying how the loss changes you, the pain of feeling alone and isolated—unable to openly mourn, unable to love and be loved by those around you.

Instead of becoming dead while you are alive, you can choose to remain open to the pain, which in large part honors the love you continue to feel for the person who died. As Colin Murray Parkes once observed, **"The pain of grief is just as much a part of life as the joy of love; it is, perhaps, the price we pay for love." In fact, your grief *is* your love.**

Paradoxically, it is gathering the courage to turn toward the pain of your grief that ultimately leads to the healing of your wounded heart. This book encourages you to be present to your multitude of thoughts and feelings, to "be with" them, for they contain the truth you are searching for, the energy you may be lacking, and the unfolding of your healing. It may be helpful to keep in mind that you will need *all* of your thoughts and feelings to lead you there, not just the feelings you judge acceptable. For it is in being honest with yourself that you find your way through the wilderness and identify the places that need and deserve your attention.

EXPRESS YOURSELF:
Go to *The Understanding Your Grief Journal* on pp. 18-19.

Setting Your Intention to Heal

You are on a journey that is naturally frightening, painful, and lonely. No words, written or spoken, can take away the pain you feel now. I hope, however, that this book will bring you some comfort and encouragement as you make a commitment to embracing that

DOSING YOUR PAIN

While this touchstone seeks to help you understand the role of pain in your healing, I want to make sure you also understand that you cannot embrace the pain of your grief in one sitting. If you were to feel it all at once, you could not survive.

Instead, **you must invite yourself to "dose" your pain—to feel it in small waves then allow it to retreat until you're ready for the next wave.** In other words, I encourage you to remember to embrace your pain a little bit at a time, then set it aside and give yourself a break, allowing time for you to restore yourself and rebuild your energy to attend to your grief again. For example, you might intentionally dose yourself with your pain for a few minutes or an hour or so once or twice each day in the coming weeks, then intentionally engage yourself in another activity that you find relaxing, pleasurable, distracting, or immersive.

I also call this back-and-forth of grief and respite "encounter—evade." You intentionally encounter your grief for a while, then you evade it until you're ready to encounter again.

Of course, you won't be able to completely escape your pain; even when you're not giving it your full attention, it will always be there, in the background, and it may forcefully break through to your other activities at any time. (I call this a "griefburst," and we'll talk more about it on p. 116.) But you cannot and shouldn't expect yourself to give the pain of your grief your full attention all the time. Befriending pain is fatiguing, difficult work, so it's absolutely essential to replenish your energy as often and as fully as you can.

very pain.

It takes a true commitment to heal your grief. Yes, you are changed, but with commitment and intention you can and will become whole again. Commitment goes hand-in-hand with the concept of "setting your intention." Intention is defined as being conscious of what you want to experience. A close cousin to "affirmation," it is using the power of positive, focused thought to produce a desired result.

> *"Believe that life is worth living, and your belief will help you create the fact."*
>
> William James

We often use the power of intention in our everyday lives. If you have an important presentation at work, for example, in the days before the presentation you might focus your thoughts on speaking clearly and confidently. You might envision yourself being well-received by your colleagues. You have set your intention to succeed in this presentation. By contrast, if you focus on the many ways your presentation can fail and you succumb to your anxiety, you are much less likely to give a good presentation.

How can you use the power of intention in your journey through grief? By setting your intention to heal.

When you set your intention to heal, you make a true commitment to positively influence the course of your journey. You choose between being what I call a "passive witness" or an "active participant" in your grief. I'm sure you have heard this tired cliché: Time heals all wounds. Yet time alone has little to do with healing. To heal, you must be willing to learn about the mystery of the grief journey. It can't be fixed or "resolved;" it can only be soothed and reconciled through actively engaging with and expressing your many thoughts and feelings.

The concept of intention-setting presupposes that your outer reality is in part a reflection of your inner thoughts and beliefs. If you can change or mold some of your thoughts and beliefs, then you can influence your reality. And in journaling and speaking (and praying and meditating on, etc.) your intentions, you help "set" them.

You might tell yourself, "I can and will reach out for support in my grief. I will become filled with hope that I can and will survive this loss." Together with these words, you might form mental pictures of hugging and talking to your friends and seeing your happier self in the future.

Setting your intention to heal is not only a way of surviving your loss (although it is indeed that!), it is also a way of guiding your grief to the most meaningful future. Of course, you will still have to honor and embrace your pain during this time. By honoring the presence of your pain, by understanding the appropriateness of your pain, you are committing to facing the pain. You are committing to paying attention to your anguish in ways that allow you to begin to breathe life into your soul again. That is a very good reason to give attention to your intention. **The alternative would be to shut down in an effort to avoid and deny your pain, which is to die while you are still alive.**

In this book, I will attempt to teach you to gently and lovingly face and experience the pain of your grief. To not be so reticent to express your grief. To not be ashamed of your tears and profound feelings of sadness. To not pull down the blinds that shut out light and love. Slowly and in doses, you can and will return to life and begin to live again in ways that put the stars back into your sky.

RECONCILING YOUR GRIEF

In addition to healing, an important concept to keep in mind as you read this book and journey through grief is that of reconciliation. You cannot "get over," "recover from," or "resolve" your grief, but you can reconcile yourself to it. That is, you can learn to incorporate it into your being and proceed with meaning and purpose in your life. Touchstone Nine is dedicated to the concept and goal of reconciliation.

EXPRESS YOURSELF:
Go to *The Understanding Your Grief Journal* on pp. 20-21.

Making Grief Your Friend

You cannot heal without mourning, which is expressing your grief outwardly. Denying your grief, running from it, or minimizing it will only make it more confusing and overwhelming. To lessen your hurt, you must embrace it. As strange as it may seem, you must make it your friend.

When I reflect on making grief my friend, I think about my father. Sometimes when I fully acknowledge that I'll never see my father physically on this earth again, I am engulfed by an overwhelming sadness. Then, with intention, I try to give attention to what comes next. Yes, I feel his absence, but I also feel his presence. I realize that while my father has been dead for many years now, my love and admiration for him have only continued to grow, undeterred by the loss of his physical presence. My intention has been, and continues

SPIRITUAL PESSIMISM VERSUS SPIRITUAL OPTIMISM

In grief, you can choose to be a spiritual pessimist or optimist. I recommend the latter.

What I mean by this is that it's up to you to decide how you will imagine your future and the beliefs that will guide you there.

For example, I have known grievers who have felt that if and when they experienced joy, they were somehow being disloyal to the person who died. This is a spiritually pessimistic belief, and it is one they are choosing, whether they know it or not. Spiritual optimists, conversely, opt to believe that they can continue to mourn and love the person who died while at the same time striving to live the remainder of their own precious days with purpose and joy.

Purposefully and regularly set your intention to be a spiritual optimist, and marvel at what happens.

to be, to honor his presence while acknowledging his absence. The beauty of this is that even as I mourn, I can continue to love.

EXPRESS YOURSELF:
Go to *The Understanding Your Grief Journal* on p. 22.

No Rewards for Speed

Reconciling your grief does not happen quickly or efficiently. "Grief work" may be some of the hardest work you ever do. Because mourning is work, it calls on your physical, cognitive, emotional, social, and spiritual reserves. And it takes time. A long time. And **there are no rewards for speed**.

Consequently, you must be patient with yourself. When you come to trust that the most intense pain will not last forever, it becomes tolerable. Deceiving yourself into thinking that the pain does not even exist makes it intolerable. Spiritual maturity in your grief work is attained when you embrace a paradox—to live at once in the state of encounter and surrender, to both work at and surrender to your grief.

As you come to know this paradox, you will slowly discover the soothing of your soul. Resist the need to try to figure everything out with your head, and let the paradox embrace you. You will find yourself wrapped up in a gentle peace—the peace of living in both encounter (dosing your grief work) and surrender (embracing the mystery of not totally understanding).

EXPRESS YOURSELF:
Go to *The Understanding Your Grief Journal* on p. 22.

"Doing Well" With Your Grief

In the lovely book *A Grief Observed*, C.S. Lewis wrote about his experiences after the death of his wife. He said, "An odd by-product of my loss is that I'm aware of being an embarrassment to everyone I meet…perhaps the bereaved ought to be isolated in special settlements like lepers." As Lewis so eloquently teaches, society often tends to make those of us in grief feel shame and embarrassment about our grief.

Shame is the feeling that something you are doing is bad. And you may feel that if you openly mourn, then you should be ashamed. After all, we are told to "carry on," "keep your chin up," and "keep busy." According to our culture, "doing well" with your grief often means acting "strong" and "under control." The message is that the person who is doing well is the one who seems strong, in control, and rational at all times.

> *"It does not matter how slowly you go, so long as you do not stop."*
>
> Confucius

Combined with this misconception is another one we've touched on. Society erroneously implies that if you as a grieving person openly express your feelings of grief, you are immature. If your feelings are fairly intense, you may be labeled "overly emotional." If your feelings are extremely intense, you may even be referred to as "crazy" or a "pathological mourner."

Allow me to assure you that if you are openly mourning, you are not immature, overly emotional, or crazy. But the societal messages about grief you may receive are! I often say that our culture has it backward in defining who is "doing well" in grief and who is "not doing well."

When your true personal feelings of grief are met with shame-based messages, discovering how to heal yourself becomes more difficult. If you internalize these messages encouraging repression of grief, you may even be tempted to act as if you feel better than you really do. **Ultimately, however, if you deny the emotions of your heart, you deny the essence of your life.**

EXPRESS YOURSELF:
Go to *The Understanding Your Grief Journal* on p. 23.

The Importance of Presence

The touchstone we are discussing in this chapter encourages you to open to the presence of your loss. As you journey through the wilderness of your grief, the concept of "presence" will be important in many ways.

To be present is to notice and give your attention to whatever is happening around and inside you in each moment. It is to honor and mindfully experience the now. We'll talk more about the practice of mindfulness in a later chapter, but for now let's remember that especially in the early months and years, your grief needs your mindful attention.

In addition to being an always-there, background reality in your life, your grief will sometimes strongly tug at you and ask for your attention. On any given day, you may feel especially sad. It is in such moments that your grief requires your presence. It is asking for your full attention and self-compassion. It would also benefit from a good dose of expression, as well.

A wonderful by-product of intentionally working on being present to your grief is that you will likely become more present to all facets of your life. As your capacity for mindfulness strengthens, you will find your daily life is enriched in often subtle but profound ways.

EXPRESS YOURSELF:
Go to *The Understanding Your Grief Journal* on p. 23.

Grief Is Not a Disease

You have probably already discovered that no quick fix exists for the pain you are enduring. But I promise you that if you can think, feel, and see yourself as an active participant in your healing, you will experience a renewed sense of meaning and purpose in your life. **Grief is not a disease—it is a normal part of love**. To be human means coming to know loss as part of your life. Many losses, or "little griefs," occur along life's path. And not all your losses are equally painful; they do not always disconnect you from yourself. But the death of a person you have loved is likely to leave you feeling disconnected from both yourself and the outside world.

"To suppress the grief, the pain, is to condemn oneself to a living death. Living fully means feeling fully; it means being completely one with what you are experiencing and not holding it at arm's length."

Philip Kapleau

Yet, while grief is a powerful experience, so, too, is your capacity to aid your own healing. In your willingness to: 1) read and reflect on the pages in this book; 2) complete the companion journal, at your own pace; and 3) possibly participate in a support group with fellow grief companions, you are demonstrating your commitment and setting your intention to reinvest in life while never forgetting the one you love.

I invite you to gently and in doses confront and befriend the pain of your grief. I will try with all my heart to show you how to look for the touchstones on your journey through the wilderness of grief so that your life can proceed with meaning and purpose.

EXPRESS YOURSELF:
Go to *The Understanding Your Grief Journal* on p. 24.

Attention, Compassion, and Expression

This touchstone is one of the most difficult for many grieving people to surrender to. The concept of the need to not just acknowledge but attend to and even befriend your pain is something you may find yourself naturally resisting. Yet allow me to remind you that the pain of your loss is both normal and necessary. It is a natural human response, and more than that, it is productive pain. **Your pain exists to ask for your attention, compassion, and expression because these are the very approaches that will allow you to integrate**

your grief over time and eventually heal. Besides, without the pain of grief, there would be no such thing as the joy of love.

Our culture's belief that pain is something to be avoided or immediately "fixed" is a pervasive grief misconception. We'll be overturning a dozen such misconceptions in the next chapter. Then, once we've cleared away much of the debris blocking your path into the wilderness of authentic grief and healing, we'll be able to move on to deeper truths about your unique journey.

> *"We have to do the best we can. This is our sacred human responsibility."*
>
> Albert Einstein

Dispel a Dozen Misconceptions about Grief

As you journey through the wilderness of your grief, if you befriend your pain and mourn openly and authentically, you will come to find a path that feels right for you, that is your path to integrating this loss into your life.

"Ten years, she's dead, and I still find myself some mornings reaching for the phone to call her. She could no more be gone than gravity or the moon."

Mary Karr

But beware—your path through the wilderness may be blocked by misconceptions about grief and mourning. What's more, others may use the misconceptions to try to pull you off your path. They will try to make you believe that the path you have chosen is wrong—even crazy, and that their way is better. When surrounded by people who believe in these misconceptions, you may feel a heightened sense of isolation. If the people who are closest to you are unable to emotionally and spiritually support you without judging you, I encourage you to seek out others who can.

The misconceptions, in essence, deny you your right to hurt and authentically express your grief. They often cause unrealistic expectations about the grief experience, and they may make you doubt or judge yourself unfairly.

As you read about this important touchstone, you may discover that you yourself have believed in some of the misconceptions. You may

MISCONCEPTION

A misconception is a mistaken notion you have about something—in other words, something you believe to be true but isn't. Misconceptions about grief are common in our culture because we tend not to openly mourn or validate or talk about grief and mourning. You can see how we'd have misconceptions about something as hidden away as grief has been.

also realize that people close to you embrace them. Don't condemn yourself or others if this is the case. Simply make use of any new insights you might gain to help you open your heart to your work of mourning in ways that restore the soul.

MISCONCEPTION 1:
Grief and mourning are the same thing

Perhaps you've noticed that people tend to use the words "grieving" and "mourning" interchangeably. There is an important distinction, however.

Grief is the constellation of internal thoughts and feelings we have when someone we love dies or we experience any significant life loss. In other words, grief is everything we naturally think and feel on the inside after a loss.

Think of grief as the container. It holds all of our thoughts, feelings, and images of our experience when we are bereaved. I think it's so interesting that many native cultures actually created vessels—usually baskets, pots, or bowls—that symbolically contained their grief.

Mourning, on the other hand, is when we take our inner grief and express it outside of ourselves in some way. Another way of defining mourning is "grief gone public" or "the outward expression of grief." Talking about the person who died, crying, expressing our thoughts and feelings through art or music, and celebrating special dates that held meaning for the person who died are just a few examples of mourning.

Grief comes naturally, but mourning usually takes intentional effort and commitment. It's worth it, though, because the only way to move toward fully integrating loss into our lives and eventually healing is not just by *grieving* but by *mourning*.

Mourning is active. Mourning is work. You will move toward reconciliation (see p. 177) not just by grieving but through deliberate, ongoing mourning.

A major theme of this book is rooted in the importance of openly and honestly mourning life losses, or expressing your grief outside of yourself. Over time and with the support of others, mourning allows you to come out of the dark and into the light.

Bereavement: *"to be torn apart," "to have special needs," "to be robbed"*

In the native cultures I just mentioned, people would get out their grief vessels occasionally as a way of intentionally attending to their grief. They would wisely use the vessels to help dose themselves with mourning.

WARNING: Because of this misconception, after someone you love dies, some of your friends and family members may in essence encourage you to "keep your grief to yourself." Yet if you were to take this message to heart, the disastrous result would be that all of your thoughts and feelings would stay neatly bottled up inside you. A catalyst for healing, however, can only be created when you develop the courage to mourn openly and honestly, in the presence of understanding, compassionate people who will not judge you. At times, of course, you will grieve alone; sitting in solitude with your pain is part of the work of grief as well. But expressing your grief outside of yourself is necessary if you are to slowly and gently move forward in your grief journey.

When you don't honor a death loss by acknowledging it, first to yourself and then to those around you, your grief will accumulate and compound. Then, over time, this denied or "carried" grief will emerge in all sorts of potentially harmful ways in your life, such as deep depression, chronic anxiety, physical complaints, difficulty in relationships, addictive behaviors, and more.

EXPRESS YOURSELF:
Go to *The Understanding Your Grief Journal* on pp. 26-27.

MISCONCEPTION 2:
Grief and mourning progress in predictable, orderly stages

You have probably heard of the "stages of grief." The world latched onto this concept because it's appealing to feel like there's a knowable structure to such a difficult life experience and to have some sense of control over it. If we believe that everyone grieves by going through the same stages, then death and grief become much less mysterious and fearsome. If only it were so simple! The truth is that grief is typically not orderly or predictable.

The concept of grief stages was popularized in 1969 with the publication of Elisabeth Kübler-Ross's landmark text *On Death and Dying*. In this groundbreaking book, Dr. Kübler-Ross listed the five stages of grief that she saw terminally ill patients experience in the face of their own impending deaths: denial, anger, bargaining, depression, and acceptance. However, Kübler-Ross never intended for her stages to be interpreted as a rigid, linear sequence to be followed by grieving people. Our culture, however, has done just that, and the consequences have often been disastrous.

As a grieving person, you will probably encounter others who have adopted a rigid system of beliefs about what you should and shouldn't experience in your grief journey—whether they adhere to the Kübler-Ross stages or an understanding wholly their own. And if you have internalized this misconception, you may also find yourself trying to prescribe and dictate your own grief experience as well. Instead of allowing yourself to be where you are on any given day, you may shame yourself or try to force yourself to be in a certain "stage."

For example, you may or may not experience normal grief symptoms of disorganization, fear, guilt, and explosive emotions (all of which we'll talk about in Touchstone Four) during your unique grief journey. Or you might move through one or more of these feelings, think you're "done" with it, then find yourself returning to it later on. Sometimes you may move from one predominant emotion to another in a short period of time. At other times, and perhaps more commonly, you may experience two or more emotions simultaneously.

> *"I wasn't prepared for the fact that grief is so unpredictable. It wasn't just sadness, and it wasn't linear. Somehow I'd thought that the first days would be the worst and then it would get steadily better, like getting over the flu. That's not how it was."*
>
> Meghan O'Rourke

Remember—do not try to determine where you "should" be in your grief. Just allow yourself to be naturally where you are and present to whatever you're experiencing in each moment.

Everyone mourns in different ways. Personal experience is your best teacher, and you and only you are the expert of your own grief. Don't think your goal is to move through prescribed stages. As you read further in this book, you'll find that a major theme is understanding that your grief is unique. That word means "only one." No one exactly like you ever existed before, and no one will ever be exactly like you again. On the journey to healing, the thoughts and feelings you will experience will be totally unique to you.

EXPRESS YOURSELF:
Go to *The Understanding Your Grief Journal* on pp. 28-29.

MISCONCEPTION 3:
You should move away from grief, not toward it

Our society often encourages prematurely moving away from grief instead of toward it. The result is that too many mourners either grieve in isolation or attempt to deny, suppress, or run away from their grief through various means.

During ancient times, Stoic philosophers encouraged their followers not to mourn, believing that reason and self-control were the appropriate responses to sorrow. Today you may find that some well-intentioned but uninformed relatives and friends still adhere to this long-held tradition. While the outward expression of grief is a requirement for healing, overcoming society's powerful message to repress and deny can be difficult.

As a grief counselor, I'm often asked, "How long should grief last?" This question itself is an outgrowth of our cultural impatience with grief and the desire to move people away from pain and suffering. Just a few weeks after a death, grievers are often expected to be "back to normal."

Mourners who continue to express their grief outwardly, on the other hand, are often viewed as "weak," "crazy," or "self-pitying." The subtle message is, "Suck it up and get on with your life." The disturbing result is that far too many people view grief as something to be overcome rather than experienced.

These messages, unfortunately, encourage you to repress your normal and necessary thoughts and feelings about the death of someone loved. You may find yourself refusing to cry, for example, because suffering in silence and "being strong" are considered admirable. Many people have internalized society's misconception that mourning should be done quietly, quickly, and efficiently. My hope is this doesn't happen to you.

> *"We are healed of a suffering only by experiencing it to the full."*
>
> Marcel Proust

After the death of someone loved, you also may feel pressured to respond to the polite question, "How are you?" with the benign response, "I'm fine." In essence, you are saying to the world, "I'm not mourning." Some friends, family, and coworkers may encourage this stance. Why? Because they have also internalized this misconception and don't want to think or talk about death. So if you are stoic and do not outwardly mourn, your behavior is often considered more socially acceptable.

This inhibiting collaborative pretense about mourning, however, does not meet your needs in grief. When your grief is ignored or minimized, you'll feel further isolated in your journey. Ultimately, you will experience the onset of "Am I going crazy?" syndrome (see Touchstone Six). Masking or moving away from your grief only creates anxiety, confusion, and depression. If you receive little or no social recognition of your normal, natural pain, you will probably begin to fear that your thoughts and feelings are abnormal.

Remember—society will often encourage you to prematurely move away from your grief. Instead, you must continually remind yourself that **only leaning toward the pain will give you the divine momentum you need to begin to reconcile your grief and heal**.

EXPRESS YOURSELF:
Go to *The Understanding Your Grief Journal* on pp. 30-31.

MISCONCEPTION 4:
Tears of grief are a sign of weakness

Just yesterday morning I read a lovely, personalized obituary in my local newspaper. The obituary described a man who had done many things in his life, had made many friends, and had touched the lives of countless people. He died of cancer in his 60s. At the end of the obituary, readers were invited to attend his funeral service and were instructed to bring memories and stories but NO TEARS. What a sad message to be included in the obituary, I thought.

While tears of grief are often associated with personal inadequacy and weakness, the worst thing you can do is to allow this wrongheaded notion to prevent you from crying.

Some people who care about you may, directly or indirectly, try to prevent your tears out of a well-intentioned but misguided desire to protect you and them from pain. You may hear comments like, "Tears won't bring him back" or "He wouldn't want you to cry." Yet, for many people, crying is an instinctive, helpful act of mourning. It's nature's way of releasing internal tension and stress hormones from your body. What's more, it allows you to communicate a need to be comforted. So don't let others stifle your need to mourn openly, even if it makes those around you feel helpless.

> "There is a sacredness in tears. They are not the mark of weakness but of power. They speak more eloquently than ten thousand tongues. They are the messengers of overwhelming grief, of deep contrition, and of unspeakable love."
>
> Washington Irving

Tears of grief foster genuine healing. In my experience companioning mourners, I have witnessed the transformation up close many times. Not only do people say they feel better after crying, they also look better. Tension and agitation seem to flow out of their bodies. After a good cry, they feel a little looser and less burdened.

You must be vigilant about guarding yourself against this misconception. Tears are not a sign of weakness. In fact, your capacity to share tears is an indication of your willingness to do the essential healing work of mourning.

EXPRESS YOURSELF:
Go to *The Understanding Your Grief Journal* on pp. 32-33.

MISCONCEPTION 5:

Being upset and openly mourning means you are being "weak" in your faith

Watch out for those who think that having faith and openly mourning are mutually exclusive. Sometimes people fail to remember this important wisdom teaching, straight from the Bible itself: "Blessed are those who mourn, for they shall be comforted."

Above all, grief is a spiritual journey of the heart and soul. If faith or spirituality are a part of your life, express it in ways that seem appropriate to you. If you are mad at God, be mad at God. Actually, being angry at God speaks of having a relationship with God in the first place. I've always said to myself and others, "God has been doing very well for some time now—so I think God can handle my anger."

Similarly, if you need a time-out from formal religious or spiritual practices, don't shame yourself. Going to exile for a period of time often assists in your healing. If people try to drag you to religious or spiritual services and you don't want to go, dig in your heels and tell them you'll go if and when you're ready.

In the meantime, I encourage you to tend to your spirit each day. Do whatever helps you feel present, peaceful, and one with creation. Spending a few minutes in nature is often a good way to do this. Prayer, meditation, yoga, journaling, and listening to music that is meaningful to you are other ways.

Don't let people take your grief away from you in the name of faith—but do take care of your spirit.

EXPRESS YOURSELF:
Go to *The Understanding Your Grief Journal* on p. 34.

MISCONCEPTION 6:

When someone you love dies, you only grieve and mourn for the physical absence of the person

When someone you love dies, you don't just lose that person's physical presence. As a result of the death, you may lose many other connections to yourself and the world around you. Sometimes I outline these potential ripple-effect losses as follows:

LOSS OF SELF

- *self*
  "I feel like part of me died when he died."

- *identity*
  You may have to rethink your role as husband or wife, mother or father, son or daughter, best friend, etc.

- *self-confidence*
  Some grievers experience lowered self-esteem. Naturally, you may have lost one of the people in your life who gave you confidence.

- *health*
  Physical symptoms of mourning

- *personality*
  "I just don't feel like myself…"

LOSS OF SECURITY

- *emotional security*
  An emotional source of support is now gone, causing emotional upheaval.

- *physical security*
  You may not feel as safe living in your home or community as you did before.

- *financial security*
  You may have new financial concerns or have to learn to manage finances in ways you didn't before.

- *lifestyle*
  Your lifestyle doesn't feel the same as it did before.

LOSS OF MEANING

- *goals and dreams*
  Hopes and dreams for the future can be shattered.

- *faith*
  You may question your faith or belief system.

- *will/desire to live*
  You may have questions related to future meaning in your life. You may ask, "Why go on…?"

- *joy*
  Life's most precious emotion, happiness, is naturally compromised by the death of someone we love.

Acknowledging and expressing the many ripple-effect losses the death has brought to your life will help you continue to be present to your unique grief journey.

EXPRESS YOURSELF:
Go to *The Understanding Your Grief Journal* on p. 35.

MISCONCEPTION 7:
You should try not to think about the person who died on special days like holidays, anniversaries, and birthdays

As with all things in grief, trying not to think about something that your heart and soul are tugging at you to think about is a bad idea. On special occasions such as holidays, anniversaries such as wedding dates and the day the person died, and your birthday or the birthday of the person who died, it's natural for your grief to well up inside you and spill over—even long after the event of the death.

It may seem logical that if you can only avoid thinking about the person who died on these special days—maybe you can cram your day so tight that you don't have a second to spare—then you can avoid some heartache. What I would ask you is this: Where does that heartache go if you don't let it out when it naturally arises? It doesn't disappear. It simply bides its time, patiently at first then urgently, like a caged animal pacing behind the bars.

You may have some family and friends who attempt to perpetuate this misconception. Actually, as with the natural tears of grief, people are often really trying to protect themselves from pain in the name of protecting you.

While you may feel particularly sad, vulnerable, and lonely during these times, remember—these feelings are honest expressions of the real you. It's normal to feel your grief more deeply on special days. And it's good to find ways to be present to your feelings and to express them.

To give yourself the time and energy you need to befriend your grief on special days, I suggest not overextending yourself in other ways. Don't feel you have to shop, bake, entertain, send cards, etc. if you're not feeling up to it.

Instead of avoiding these days, you may want to commemorate the life of the person who died by doing something they would have appreciated. On his birthday, what could you do to honor his special passions? On the anniversary of her death, what could you do to remember her life? You might want to spend these times in the company of people who help you feel safe and cared for and in whose company you can openly express your normal, necessary grief.

EXPRESS YOURSELF:
Go to *The Understanding Your Grief Journal* on pp. 36-37.

MISCONCEPTION 8:
At the funeral or as soon as possible, you have to say goodbye to the person who died

Our culture tends to make grievers believe that if they say goodbye to the person who died, they'll be able to close that chapter of their lives and "move on." Nothing could be further from the truth.

Actually, when it comes to grief, **funerals are more about saying hello to the new reality of a death than they are about saying goodbye. They are more a ritual of opening than of closure** ("closure," a close cousin to "goodbye," being a related major grief misconception).

And apart from the funeral, the early days and weeks of grief are all about acknowledging the reality of the death and *beginning* to live with that painful new reality. The funeral itself is also intended to help you acknowledge the reality of the death, recall the life, activate support, express grief into mourning, search for meaning, and reintegrate into your community in a changed social status.

The goodbyes to the person who died will unfold more slowly, over time. As you actively mourn in the months and years to come, you will naturally begin to feel that you have arrived at a goodbye that feels right to you. For some of you, that may be finding ways to continue to give honor to the life of your precious person who has died. For others of you it might be a temporary goodbye based on your belief that you will one day be reunited with the person who died. In this form of goodbye, many grievers fully come to terms with the separation yet carry on the relationship by continuing to speak to the person who died and feel their ongoing, if ethereal, presence.

Whatever form of goodbye you arrive at, it will naturally take a long time to fully settle into. It is not something you can do quickly or efficiently, and lots of hellos must come first.

When culturally appropriate as well as possible given the circumstances, many people in grief have told me that saying goodbye to the body of the person who died before burial or cremation was an important step for them in coming to terms with the death. If you were not able to spend time with the body, you may find you need to work more actively and intentionally on acknowledging the reality of the death before you can gain momentum in your journey through the wilderness.

EXPRESS YOURSELF:
Go to *The Understanding Your Grief Journal* on pp. 38-39.

MISCONCEPTION 9.

After someone you love dies, the goal should be to "get over" your grief as soon as possible

You may already have heard the question, "Are you over it yet?" Or, even worse, "Well, you should be over it by now!" To think that as a human being you ever "get over" your grief is a misnomer. You don't "get over" grief; you learn to live with it. You learn to integrate it into your life and the fabric of your being.

We will talk more about this important distinction in Touchstone Nine. For now, suffice it to say that **you will never "get over" your grief. As you actively engage with your grief, however, and do the work of your mourning, you can and will become reconciled to it**. Unfortunately, if the people around you expect you to "get over" your grief, they set you up to fail.

> *"Grief is forever. It doesn't go away; it becomes a part of you, step for step, breath for breath. I will never stop grieving Bailey because I will never stop loving her. That's just how it is. All I can do is love her, and love the world, emulate her by living with daring and spirit and joy."*
>
> Jandy Nelson

EXPRESS YOURSELF:
Go to *The Understanding Your Grief Journal* on pp. 40-41.

MISCONCEPTION 10:

Nobody can help you with your grief

We have all heard people say, "Nobody can help you but yourself." Or you may have been told since childhood, "If you want something done right, do it yourself." Yet, the truth is that **the most self-compassionate thing you can do for yourself at this naturally difficult time is to reach out for help from others**.

Think of it this way: Grieving and mourning may be the hardest work you have ever done. And hard work is less burdensome when others lend a hand. Life's greatest challenges—getting through school, raising children, pursuing a career—are in many ways team efforts. So it should be with mourning.

Sharing your pain with others won't make it disappear, but it will, over time, make it more bearable. By definition, mourning (i.e., the outward expression of grief) requires that you get support from sources outside of yourself. Grieving may be a solo activity, but mourning is often not. Reaching out for help also connects you to other people and strengthens the bonds of love that make life seem worth living.

"Deep grief sometimes is almost like a specific location, a coordinate on a map of time. When you are standing in that forest of sorrow, you cannot imagine that you could ever find your way to a better place. But if someone can assure you that they themselves have stood in that same place, and now have moved on, sometimes this will bring hope."

Elizabeth Gilbert

EXPRESS YOURSELF:
Go to *The Understanding Your Grief Journal* on pp. 41-42.

MISCONCEPTION 11:
If you're focusing too much on your grief, you're being selfish

As we've said, because our culture doesn't "do" death or grief very well, it tends to make us feel that our grief should be private, and, after a certain point, it shouldn't interfere with our ability to keep living our lives.

If we focus on or express our grief "too much" or for "too long," on the other hand, we're often considered weak, immature, or selfish.

I couldn't disagree more. The experience of grief and mourning after the death of a significant loved one is among the most consequential things that will ever happen to us. Not only is deep grief normal and natural in this circumstance, it's necessary. It's the only way to get from the before to the after.

Acknowledging, being present to, befriending, expressing, and even appropriately wallowing in your grief are essential life tasks for you right now. They may take up most or all of your time and energy for a while, and if they do, that's OK. It doesn't mean you're being selfish, though. On the contrary, it means you're being self-aware and self-sustaining. It also means you're reconstructing yourself so that eventually you can begin to engage with and support others again.

You've suffered a serious emotional and spiritual injury. Just as if you'd sustained a life-threatening physical injury, you need intensive care to survive in the short-term and to go on to thrive in the long-term. Do we tell a car-accident victim in critical condition in the ICU that they're being selfish? Do we suggest to a person who's recently had open-heart surgery that they need to stop whining, quit focusing on their health so much, and get back to "normal"? Of course not!

So if you're focusing a lot on your own grief and mourning right now, forgive yourself. You're not being selfish—you're being courageous, and you're doing hard, necessary work.

EXPRESS YOURSELF:
Go to *The Understanding Your Grief Journal* on pp. 43-44.

MISCONCEPTION 12:
When grief and mourning are finally reconciled, they never come up again

If only this were so. As your experience has probably already taught you, grief comes in and out like waves from the ocean. Sometimes when you least expect it, a huge wave comes along and pulls your feet right out from under you.

Heightened periods of sadness can overwhelm us when we're in grief—even years after a death. These moments can seem to come out of nowhere and can be frightening and painful. Something as simple as a sound, a smell, or a phrase can bring on what I call a "griefburst." My dad loved Frank Sinatra's music. I experience a griefburst almost every time I hear Frank's voice.

Allow yourself to experience griefbursts without shame or self-judgment, no matter where or when they occur. Sooner or later, one will probably happen when you're surrounded by other people, maybe even strangers. If you would feel more comfortable, retreat to somewhere more private, or go see someone you know will understand. (For more on griefbursts, see p. 116.)

You will always, for the rest of your life, feel some grief over this death. It will no longer dominate your life, but it will always be there reminding you of the love you have for the person who died.

"You don't go around grieving all the time, but the grief is still there and always will be."

Nigella Lawson

EXPRESS YOURSELF:
Go to *The Understanding Your Grief Journal* on pp. 44-45.

Keep in mind that the misconceptions about grief and mourning explored in this chapter are certainly not all the misconceptions about grief and mourning. Use the space provided in *The Understanding Your Grief Journal* (p. 46) to note any other grief misconceptions you have encountered since the death of someone loved.

Realistic Expectations for Grief and Mourning

My hope is that as we conclude Touchstone Two, you will find it helpful to list some appropriate "conceptions" of grief. These are the honest, authentic realities you *can* hold onto as you journey toward healing.

1. Grief is internal. Mourning is external. You will naturally grieve, but you will probably have to make a conscious, intentional, and regular effort to mourn.

2. Your grief will be unpredictable, and it will not likely progress in an orderly fashion. What's more, it will involve a wide variety of different thoughts and feelings.

3. You must welcome your grief and make it your friend. You need

to feel it to heal it. Also, even as you're working to befriend your grief, it will probably hurt more before it hurts less.

4. Crying and all forms of expression of grief and mourning are signs of strength.

5. Having faith and experiencing deep grief can go hand-in-hand.

6. When someone you love dies, you not only suffer the loss of their physical presence, you also experience any number of ripple-effect losses. Your grief and mourning will impact you in all five realms of experience: physically, cognitively, emotionally, socially, and spiritually.

7. Special days like holidays, anniversaries, and birthdays naturally arouse your grief and are excellent times to mourn openly and seek support from others.

8. You have to say "hello" to your grief and all of your thoughts and feelings of loss—a process that takes a long time—before you can begin to find ways to say goodbye to the chapter of your life that is now over.

9. You will never "get over" your grief. Instead, you will learn to live with it.

10. You need other people to help you with and through your grief. You must accept their support, and you must also reach out for support.

11. Spending time and energy focusing on and expressing your grief is essential self-care. It's hard, necessary work.

12. You will always grieve for the person who died, and you will probably experience griefbursts forever. But if you mourn openly and thoroughly in doses for as long as it takes, your grief will soften over time. You will not always feel this bad.

When you are surrounded by people who can distinguish the

misconceptions of grief from these realities, you can and will experience the support you need and deserve. Usually, the capacity to bear witness to and affirm normal, necessary grief and mourning is most present in people who have been on a grief journey themselves and are willing to be with you during this difficult time.

EXPRESS YOURSELF:

Go to *The Understanding Your Grief Journal* on pp. 47-49.

TOUCHSTONE THREE

Embrace the
Uniqueness of Your Grief

The wilderness of your grief is *your* wilderness—it is a creation of your unique self, the unique person who died, the unique relationship you shared, and the unique circumstances of your life. Your wilderness may be rockier or more level than that of others. Your path may be revealed in a straight line, or, more likely, it may be full of twists and turns. In your wilderness, you will encounter places that are meaningful only to you, and you will experience the topography in your own way.

> *"Our grief is as individual as our lives."*
>
> Dr. Elisabeth Kübler-Ross

In the course of human life, everyone experiences loss. But our grief journeys are never precisely the same. Despite what you may hear about grief stages or what you should or should not be thinking/feeling/doing, **you will grieve and do the work of mourning in your own singular way.** Be careful about comparing your experience with that of other people. Do not adopt assumptions about how long your grief should last or how you're "measuring up." Instead, consider taking a one-day-at-a-time approach. This will give you the permission and grace you need you to mourn at your own pace and in your own way.

This touchstone invites you to explore some of the unique reasons your grief is what it is—the "whys" of your particular journey through the wilderness. The "whys" that follow are not all the "whys" in the world, of course, just some of the most common. As you write out your responses in your companion journal, I believe you will discover a deeper understanding of and appreciation for the uniqueness of your grief.

WHY 1:
Your Relationship with the Person Who Died

Your relationship with the person who died was different than that person's relationship with anyone else. For example, if your spouse died, you may have been soulmates as well as husband or wife. Or perhaps the person who died was a close friend whom you loved but also had frequent disagreements or divisive conflicts with. Or maybe you were separated by physical distance from a family member or friend who died, so you weren't as close emotionally as you would have liked, yet you find yourself grieving deeply.

In general, **the stronger your attachment to the person who died, the more difficult your grief journey will be**. It only makes sense that the closer you felt to the person who died, the more torn apart you will feel after the death. Ambivalent, rocky relationships can also be particularly hard to integrate after a death. You may feel a strong sense of "unfinished business"—things you wanted to say but never did, conflicts you wanted to resolve but didn't.

Whatever the nature and circumstances of your relationship, you are the best person to describe them. As you work on remembering, understanding, and honoring your relationship with the person who died, you will be mourning this central truth of the loss and giving yourself momentum toward healing.

SOULMATE GRIEF

Soulmates are any two people who share a particularly deep affinity and connection. Spouses and life partners may be soulmates, but soulmates can also be parent and child, siblings, or close friends. Again, what matters is the strength and qualities of the bond in the relationship. The shorthand soulmates often use to describe one another is "the love of my life."

If your soulmate has died, your grief journey is likely to be especially painful and difficult—more challenging than any other grief you've experienced in your life. Your wilderness may be particularly remote and severe. If this is the case for you, I invite you to also look into my book *When Your Soulmate Dies: A Guide to Healing Through Heroic Mourning*. The concept of heroic mourning will offer you additional support and encouragement as you journey forward.

EXPRESS YOURSELF:
Go to *The Understanding Your Grief Journal* on pp. 52-55.

WHY 2:

The Circumstances of the Death

How, why, and when the person you love died has a significant influence on your journey into grief. For example, was the death sudden or anticipated? How old was the person who died? Do you feel you might have been able to prevent the death?

EXPECTED LOSS AND ANTICIPATORY GRIEF

If you are reading this book, you have probably suffered a significant loss that has already happened. For some of you it may have been a death that you had been anticipating, perhaps for a long time.

If you love someone who suffered from dementia or another terminal illness, for example, you naturally began to anticipate their eventual death and your coming grief long before the day of their death. You also experienced the griefs of all the incremental losses along the way. Other common causes of anticipatory grief are advanced age in someone you love, a coming separation or divorce, pending major medical issues or procedures, and upcoming major life transitions, such as a job change or relocation.

Anticipatory grief is often a dark, painful, and confusing time of limbo. If you experienced anticipatory grief before the death, that "pre-grief" is part of the terrain of your grief wilderness as well. As you read through the touchstones in this book and complete the corresponding journaling exercises, I invite you to give consideration to both your anticipatory and current grief. Yet anticipatory grief also has its own unique features. If you would like to learn more or are anticipating a significant loss to come, I encourage you to read my short book *Expected Loss: Coping with Anticipatory Grief* in addition to this one.

A sudden, unexpected death obviously does not allow you any opportunity to prepare yourself for what was about to happen. But are you ever "ready" for that moment at all? After a death due to terminal illness, friends and family members often tell me that they were still, in a sense, shocked by the death. I know this was my experience when my dad died. However, I did feel fortunate that I was able to share special time with him before he died and that we had ample opportunity to tell one another how we felt.

The age of the person who died also affects your feelings about the death. Within the natural order of things, we anticipate that parents will die before their children do. But when a child dies, this understanding of what is right is turned upside-down. Or your grief might be heightened when a middle-aged person dies in what was thought to be the prime of their life. Basically, we often find our grief easier when we feel that the person who died had a chance to live out a long, full life. When we feel that a life was cut short, our innate sense of injustice colors our grief.

You may also be asking yourself if you could have done anything to prevent the death. "If only I had gotten him to the doctor sooner," you may be thinking. Or, "If only I had driven instead of her." These kinds of "if-onlys" are natural for you to explore, even if there is no logical way in which you are actually responsible for the death. What you're really feeling, at bottom, is a lack of control over what happened. And accepting that we have little control over the lives of those we love is a difficult thing indeed.

EXPRESS YOURSELF:
Go to *The Understanding Your Grief Journal* on pp. 56-58.

WHY 3:
The People in Your Life

Mourning is the outward expression of grief. Part of the benefit of mourning comes from the routine act of moving your grief from the inside to the outside—over and over again, as often as you need to. But the other part is that mourning serves as a signal to the people in your life that you're hurting and you need their empathy and support.

You need that empathy and support to heal. **Without a stabilizing support system of at least one other person, odds are you will have difficulty reconciling your grief.** Healing requires an environment of empathy, caring, and gentle encouragement.

> *"The friend who can be silent with us in a moment of despair or confusion, who can stay with us in an hour of grief and bereavement, who can tolerate not knowing...not healing, not curing... that is a friend who cares."*
>
> Henri Nouwen

Just because you have family and friends doesn't mean you're necessarily well-supported, though. For example, you may have people in your life whom you are ostensibly close to, but since your loss you may have discovered that they have little compassion or patience for you and your grief. If so, a vital ingredient for healing is missing. Or you might have some friends and relatives who were supportive right after the death but who stopped supporting you soon after. Again, for healing to occur, social support must be ongoing.

Keep in mind that if your core support group is made up of people who themselves are also grieving this death, you may all experience what I call the "pressure-cooker phenomenon." Everyone may need support at the same time, and because you are all grieving, each of you also has a naturally lowered capacity to be understanding of others. This can result in heightened tension, misunderstandings, bickering, outbursts, hurt feelings, and more. If the pressure-cooker phenomenon is making it hard for you to find someone who will listen to you without judging and without monopolizing the conversation with their own grief (though equal sharing of conversation time is appropriate), try turning to friends and family who live farther away or are more emotionally distant from this particular death. If you're comfortable with technology, online grief forums can also be helpful.

And finally, you yourself are part of this support equation. Even when you have a solid support system in place, do you find that you are willing and able to accept the support? If you're ashamed of your need to mourn or mistakenly believe that you can do it all on your own, you may end up isolating yourself from the very people who could support you in your journey through grief.

EXPRESS YOURSELF:
Go to *The Understanding Your Grief Journal* on pp. 59-62.

IS YOUR GRIEF COMPLICATED?

All grief is complex and challenging, but sometimes certain losses and life experiences give rise to "complicated grief."

Complicated grief is simply normal grief that has been made extra difficult by certain circumstances, such as violent, premature, or ambiguous causes of death; concurrent mental health challenges in the mourner; a history of abuse or addiction in the relationship; other simultaneous, major stressors in the mourner's life; and many more. Complicated grief in the aftermath of a traumatic event is also called "traumatic grief."

We'll be talking more about complicated grief in Touchstone Eight, but in the meantime, if it seems your grief and life circumstances are totally overwhelming, or if you feel stuck, in constant despair, or unable to function in your day-to-day life, you may be experiencing complicated or traumatic grief. If this is the case for you, I urge you to reach out for help right away from your primary-care provider as well as a compassionate grief counselor.

Rest assured that you're not ill, and you don't have a disorder. Rather, you're experiencing a normal response to an abnormally difficult situation—one that would likely overwhelm anyone's capacity to cope. You have severe symptoms because you've suffered a severe injury. So please—get the immediate, intensive care you need and deserve.

WHY 4:

Your Unique Personality

What words would you use to describe yourself? What adjectives do other people use to describe you? Are you serious? Silly? Friendly? Shy?

> *"Grief does not change you. It reveals you."*
>
> John Green

Whatever your unique personality, rest assured it will be reflected in your grief. For example, if you are quiet by nature, you may express your grief quietly. If you are outgoing, you may be more naturally expressive with your grief.

How you have responded to other losses or crises in your life will likely also be consistent with how you respond to this death. If you tend to remain distant or run away from crises, you may do the same thing now. If, however, you have always confronted challenges head-on and openly expressed your thoughts and feelings, you may now follow that pattern of behavior.

Other aspects of your personality—such as your self-esteem, values, and beliefs—also impact your response to the death. In addition, any preexisting mental health history will probably influence your grief as well.

EXPRESS YOURSELF:
Go to *The Understanding Your Grief Journal* on pp. 62-64.

WHY 5:

The Unique Personality of the Person Who Died

Just as your own personality is reflected in your grief journey, so, too, is the unique personality of the person who died. What was the person who died like? What role(s) did they play in your life? Was he the funny one? Or was she the responsible one?

Really, personality is the sum total of all the characteristics that made this person who they were. The way she talked, the way he smiled, the way she ate her food, the way he worked—all these and so many more little things go into creating personality. It's no wonder there's so much to miss and that grief is so complex when all these mannerisms and ways of being are gone all at once.

> *"After (her) death I began to see her as she had really been. It was less like losing someone than discovering someone."*
>
> Nancy Halle

Whatever you loved most about the person who died, that is what you will now likely miss the most. And paradoxically, whatever you liked least about the person who died is what may trouble you the most now. If, for example, your father was a cold, uncaring person, after his death you may find yourself struggling even more with his apparent lack of love. You may have always wished you could change this aspect of his personality, but now that he is gone, you know with finality that you can't.

Whatever your feelings are about the unique life and personality of the person who died, talk about them openly. The key is finding someone you can trust who will listen to you without judging or constantly giving advice.

EXPRESS YOURSELF:
Go to *The Understanding Your Grief Journal* on pp. 65-70.

WHY 6:
Your Cultural Background

Your cultural background is an important part of how you experience and express your grief. Sometimes it's hard for modern-day North Americans to articulate what their cultural background is. "My mother is half Irish, a quarter Mexican and a quarter I don't know what," you might say. "And my father comes from a strong Italian family." So what does that make you? And how does this mixture influence your grief?

When I say culture, I actually mean the values, rules (spoken and unspoken), and traditions that guide you and your family. Often these values, rules, and traditions have been handed down generation after generation and are shaped by the ethnicities or areas of the world your family originally came from. Your cultural background is also shaped by education and political beliefs (religion, too, but we'll get to that in a minute).

Basically, your culture is your way of being in the world.

EXPRESS YOURSELF:
Go to *The Understanding Your Grief Journal* on pp. 70-72.

WHY 7:
Your Religious or Spiritual Background

Your personal belief system can have a tremendous impact on your journey into grief. You may discover that your religious or spiritual life is deepened, renewed, or changed as a result of your loss. Or you may well find yourself questioning your beliefs as part of your work of mourning.

When someone loved dies, some people may feel very close to God or a higher power, while others may feel more distant or even hostile. You may find yourself asking questions such as, "Why has this happened to me?" or "What is the meaning of this?" While this search for meaning is necessary, you may not find neat, satisfying answers to all of your questions about faith or spirituality.

The word "faith" means to believe in something for which there is no proof. For some people, faith means believing in and following a set of religious rules. For others, faith is a belief in God or a spirit or a force that is greater than we are.

Mistakenly, some people think that with faith, there is no need to mourn. If you internalize this misconception, you will set yourself up to grieve internally but not mourn externally. Even if you have faith, you still have the right and the need to mourn! If you are grieving, you need to mourn those normal, necessary thoughts and feelings outside of yourself, period—regardless of your faith.

As part of your search for meaning (more about this on p. 104), you will probably find yourself reevaluating your life based on this loss. You will need compassionate friends who are willing to listen to you as you explore your religious or spiritual values, question your attitude toward life, and renew your resources for living. You may also want to seek out religious or spiritual leaders or mentors to have such conversations with. This process takes time, and it can lead to possible changes in your religious or spiritual values, beliefs, and lifestyle.

EXPRESS YOURSELF:
Go to *The Understanding Your Grief Journal* on pp 72-74.

WHY 8:
Other Crises or Stresses in Your Life Right Now

What else is going on in your life right now? Although we often think it shouldn't, the earth does keep turning after the death of someone loved. You may still have to work and manage finances. Other people in your life may be sick or in need of help of some kind. You may have children or elderly parents to care for (or both!). You may have too many commitments and too little time and energy to complete them.

Whatever your specific situation, I'm sure that your grief is not the only stress in your life right now. And the more intense and numerous the other current stresses in your life, the more overwhelming your grief journey may be.

If at all possible, take steps to de-stress your life for the time being. Give up optional obligations, and defer any unnecessary projects. Now is the time to concentrate on mourning and being self-compassionate.

EXPRESS YOURSELF:
Go to *The Understanding Your Grief Journal* on pp. 74-76.

WHY 9:
Your Experiences with Loss and Death in the Past

One way to think about yourself is that you are the sum total of all that you have experienced in your life so far. Your consciousness is in large part a creation of what you do and what happens to you. Before this death, you may have experienced other significant losses in your life. Did anyone close to you die before? What was that death and subsequent grief journey like for you? How did it affect your

TOO MUCH LOSS

Grief overload is what you may feel when you experience too many significant losses all at once or in a relatively short period of time.

The grief of loss overload is different from typical grief because it is emanating from more than one loss and because it is jumbled. Our minds and hearts have enough trouble coping with one loss at a time, but when they have to deal with multiple losses simultaneously, the grief often seems especially chaotic and defeating. Before you can mourn one loss, here comes another loss. Even if you have coped with grief effectively in the past, you may be finding that this time it's different. This time you may feel like you're struggling to survive.

If you have suffered multiple losses and are struggling with grief overload, I encourage you to work with a grief counselor. Even if you have empathetic friends and listeners in your life, you need and deserve extra support. An experienced, compassionate grief counselor can help you create a plan for sorting and mourning the separate losses. Each will need its own time and attention, and a counselor can help you navigate the process in ways you will find helpful.

To learn more about grief overload, please also see my book *Too Much Loss: Coping with Grief Overload.*

expectations for future deaths in your life? Have you found those expectations to be true this time?

The more "experienced" you are with death, the less shocked you may feel this time around. Often people find that the more deaths they mourn, and the older they get, the more natural the cycle of life seems to them. This is not to say that they aren't sad and don't need to mourn, for they are and they do. But it is to say that they begin to integrate death and loss more seamlessly into living.

Conversely, you may be finding that even if you have a lot of experience with loss, this death is hitting you harder. You might feel surprised at the intensity of your grief. Rest assured that grief can be unpredictable like that, and work toward integrating your grief as it comes. The more you befriend it, the more you may come to some understanding of why it is feeling more intense this time around.

Other non-death losses in your past may also influence your grief journey. Divorce, job loss, financial downturns, severed relationships—all these can affect your worldview as well as your capacity to cope now.

EXPRESS YOURSELF:
Go to *The Understanding Your Grief Journal* on pp. 76-77.

WHY 10:
Your Physical and Mental Health

How you feel physically and mentally has a significant effect on your grief. If you are tired and eating poorly, your coping skills will be diminished. If you were dealing with physical or mental health issues before the death, your symptoms may now be worse.

"I don't know why they call it heartbreak. It feels like every part of my body is broken, too."

Chloe Woodward

We'll discuss this important issue further in Touchstone Seven. For now, bear in mind that taking care of yourself physically and mentally is one of the best things you can do to lay the foundation for healthy mourning.

EXPRESS YOURSELF:
Go to *The Understanding Your Grief Journal* on p. 78.

WHY 11:
Your Gender

Gender norms and social constructs may not only influence your grief but also the ways in which others relate to you at this time.

Historically, men in Western cultures have been encouraged and expected to be "strong" and restrained, for example. As a result, they have often had more difficulty in allowing themselves to embrace and express painful feelings and accept support. Women, on the other hand, have been discouraged from expressing anger but expected to cry and show vulnerability.

Thank goodness these walls are crumbling. As our cultural understanding of gender and gender norms is evolving, grieving people are getting to be grieving people—and that is as it should be. Your feelings are your feelings, regardless of your sex or gender identification. And I believe all people are born with the instinct to grieve and mourn.

But because most of us have also, over the course of our lives, internalized deep-seated cultural stereotypes about gender and emotions, I simply ask that you try to become aware of them, especially if and when they may be hindering your capacity to be present to your genuine grief and express it authentically, without shame or self-judgment.

EXPRESS YOURSELF:
Go to *The Understanding Your Grief Journal* on pp. 79-80.

WHY 12:
The Ritual or Funeral Experience

Funerals and memorial services for someone you love can either help or hinder your personal grief experience. There is no single, right way to have a funeral. We do know, however, that holding a meaningful ritual for survivors can aid in their social, emotional, and spiritual healing after a death.

"The biggest problem is the funerals that don't exist. People call the funeral home, they pick up the body, they mail the ashes to you, no grief, not happiness, no remembrance, no nothing. That happens more often than it doesn't in the United States."

Caitlin Doughty

Funerals are a time and a place to express your feelings about the death. The funeral also can serve as a time to honor the person who died, bring you closer to others who can give you needed support, affirm that life goes on even in the face of death, and give you a context of meaning that is in keeping with your own religious, spiritual, or philosophical background. **In short, a good funeral can help put you on a good path to healing.**

If you were unable to attend the funeral of the person who died, or if the funeral was minimized, distorted, or nonexistent, you may find that this complicates your grief experience. Be assured, however, that it is never too late after a death to plan and carry out a ritual (even a second or third ceremony) that will help meet your needs. For example, you might choose to have a tree-planting ceremony in the spring in honor of the person who died. Or you might elect to hold a memorial service on the anniversary of the death. The power of ceremony is that it helps people heal. You deserve ceremony, and so do the other people

THE IMPORTANCE OF TELLING YOUR STORY

A vital part of healing in grief is often "telling the story" over and over again.

The story of the life of the person who died, the times you shared, and their death comprises many or all of the "whys" we've been reviewing in this touchstone. I find that the two major backward-looking "whys" that grievers naturally give attention to are their relationship with the person who died and the circumstances of the death. But your story may include bits of all the "whys" and other things as well.

It's normal and necessary to tell this story. The more you tell it, the more it starts to come together into a coherent narrative with a beginning, middle, and end. The more you tell it, the deeper your acknowledgment of the loss becomes and the more you begin to discover some level of understanding and reconciliation with what happened.

What if you don't want to talk about it? It's OK to respect this self-protective feeling for a while, but at some point you will probably be well served to start talking about it. Keeping your thoughts and feelings about the death inside you only makes them more powerful. Over time, your grief story will likely evolve from one dominated by the death to one dominated by memories of the person who died. This is a natural progression and a sign that you are you are integrating the loss into your life.

Find people who are willing to listen to you tell your story, over and over again if necessary, without judgment. But remember that not everyone has the capacity to be an empathetic listener. Seek out listeners who can be present to your pain and who don't mind if you need to repeat yourself often in the days, weeks, and months ahead.

mourning this death. For more on the power of ritual to facilitate mourning, see page 105.

EXPRESS YOURSELF:
Go to *The Understanding Your Grief Journal* on pp. 80-82.

What else has shaped your unique grief journey? There are probably other factors, large and small, that are influencing your grief right now. What are they? I invite you to think about them and to write about them in your companion journal.

EXPRESS YOURSELF:
Go to *The Understanding Your Grief Journal* on p. 83.

Moving from Whys to Whats

My hope is that Touchstone Three has helped you understand why your grief is being experienced the way it is. But what is even more fundamental for you to be attuned to is what your thoughts and feelings are. What are you feeling today? What have you been thinking about for the last day or two?

A big part of healing in grief is learning to listen and attend to your inner voice and to give those thoughts and feelings expression as you experience them. In the next chapter we will discuss some of these common and varied feelings.

Explore Your
Feelings of Loss

On your journey through the wilderness of your grief, a critical trail marker to be on the watch for is Touchstone Four, which guides you in exploring your many and varied feelings of loss. Actually, this fourth touchstone colors all the others, because your emotions shape what each of the other touchstones *feel like* for you.

> *"Did you ever know, dear, how much you took away with you when you left? I was wrong to say the stump was recovering from the amputation. I was deceived because it has so many ways to hurt me that I discover them only one by one."*
>
> C.S. Lewis

So far on the path to healing we've explored opening to the presence of your loss, dispelling common misconceptions about grief, and embracing the uniqueness of your grief. The primary way in which you experience these touchstones is by how they feel for you. Opening to the presence of your loss creates pain and feels hurtful. It may also make you feel numb, angry, fatigued, and more. Dispelling the common misconceptions about grief may cause you to feel relief and/or confusion. And embracing the uniqueness of your grief can feel affirming and may ultimately give you a profound sense of peace.

As strange as your emotions might seem, they are a true expression of where you are in your grief journey at any given moment. Rather than deny or feel victimized by your feelings, I hope to help you learn to tune into and learn from them. Naming the feelings and acknowledging them are the first steps to integrating them. In fact, it's actually this process of becoming acquainted and friendly with your feelings that will help you heal.

My goal in this touchstone is to help you see how normal your grief thoughts, feelings, and behaviors are. I have companioned thousands of grieving people, and they have taught me about many, many different thoughts and feelings after a death. Rest assured that while in one sense your specific thoughts and feelings are completely unique to you, broadly they are also usually a common, understandable human response to loss. Questions throughout this section of your companion journal will encourage you to consider if a particular feeling I am describing is, or has been, a part of your grief. Moreover, keep in mind that although you may not have experienced some of these thoughts and feelings so far, you may in the months and years to come.

EXPRESS YOURSELF:
Go to *The Understanding Your Grief Journal* on pp. 86.

Shock, Numbness, Denial, and Disbelief

Thank goodness for shock, numbness, and disbelief! Other words that mourners use to describe their initial grief experience are "dazed" and "stunned." These feelings are nature's way of temporarily protecting you from the full reality of the death. They help insulate you psychologically until you are more able to tolerate what you don't want to believe. In essence, these feelings serve as a temporary time-out or psychic shock absorber.

Especially in the beginning of your grief journey, your emotions need time to catch up with what your mind has been told. On one level, you know the person is dead. But on other, deeper levels, you aren't yet able or willing to truly believe it or totally understand it. This mixture of shock, numbness, and disbelief acts as an anesthetic: The pain exists, but you may not fully feel it. Typically, a physiological component also accompanies feelings of shock. Your autonomic nervous system is affected and may cause physical symptoms such as heart palpitations, queasiness, stomach pain, and dizziness.

During your period of shock, you may find yourself hysterically crying, having angry outbursts, or even laughing or fainting. Rest assured that these are all normal responses to a life-altering experience. Unfortunately, some people may try to squelch these behaviors, believing them to be hysterical or out-of-control.

They may try to quiet you in an effort to feel more comfortable themselves. But the reality is that this is an out-of-control, uncomfortable time for you. Trying to control yourself would mean suppressing your instinctive response to the loss. Remember—your needs are the priority right now, not theirs. Do what you need to do to survive.

"At times it feels like being mildly drunk, or concussed. There is a sort of invisible blanket between the world and me. I find it hard to take in what anyone says."

C.S. Lewis

Short-term memory is also affected by shock. You may not remember specific words being spoken to you. Your mind is blocking; it hears but cannot listen well. Although you may not remember some, or most, of the words others are sharing with you, you may well remember that you felt comforted. Their nonverbal presence is probably more important to you than anything they might say. As Maya Angelou wisely said, "I've learned that people will forget what you said, people will forget what you did, but people will never forget how you made them feel." This is never more true than in the early weeks of grief.

You may also feel a sense of surrealness and distance from what is happening around you. Some degree of dissociation in early grief is common. This is when you feel like you're there but not there, or that you're disconnected from the experiences that you're right in the middle of. "It feels like a dream," people in early grief often say. "I feel like I might wake up and none of this will have happened." They also say, "I was there, but yet I really wasn't. I managed to do what needed to be done, but I didn't feel a part of it."

Even after you have moved beyond shock, numbness, and disbelief, don't be surprised if these feelings resurface. Birthdays, anniversaries, and other special occasions that may be known only to you often trigger shock that this person you love so very much is no longer there to share these days with.

Denial is common, too, and is one of the most misunderstood aspects of the grief journey. Temporarily, denial, like shock and numbness, is a great gift. It helps you survive the early days and weeks. However, your denial should soften over time as you actively mourn and begin to acknowledge, slowly and in doses, that the person you love is truly dead. While denial is helpful—even necessary—early in your grief, ongoing denial clearly blocks the path to healing. If you cannot fully acknowledge the reality of the death, you can never mourn it.

Usually in grief, denial goes on at one level of awareness while acknowledgment of the reality of the death goes on at another level. Your mind may approach and retreat from the reality of the death over and over again as you try to embrace and integrate the meaning of the death into your life. As I mentioned in Touchstone One, this back-and-forth, evade—encounter seesaw is normal. The key is not to get stuck on evade.

SELF-CARE GUIDELINES

A critical point to realize is that shock, numbness, denial, and disbelief are not feelings you should try to prevent yourself from experiencing. Instead, be thankful that this shock absorber is available at a time when you need it most. Be compassionate with yourself. Allow for and surrender to this instinctive form of self-protection. This dimension of grief provides a much-needed, albeit temporary, means of survival.

A primary self-care principle during this time is to reach out for support from caring friends, family, and caregivers you trust. When you are in shock, your instinctive response is to need other people to care for you. Let them. Allow yourself to be nurtured.

Accepting support does not mean being totally passive and doing nothing for yourself, though. Actually, having others take over completely is usually not helpful. Given appropriate support and understanding, you will find value in doing for yourself what you can. In other words, don't allow anyone to do for you what you *want* to do for yourself.

A few misguided people may try to talk you out of your denial. They will make comments like, "You just have to admit what's happened." While your ultimate healing does require acknowledging the reality of the death, this period of shock and numbness is probably not the time to try to embrace the full depth of your loss. If others insist on taking away your temporary or intermittent need to deny the death, I suggest that you ignore or avoid them.

EXPRESS YOURSELF:
Go to your *Understanding Your Grief Journal* on pp. 87-89.

Disorganization, Confusion, Searching, and Yearning

Perhaps the most isolating and frightening part of your grief journey is the sense of disorganization, confusion, searching, and yearning that often comes with the loss. These feelings frequently arise when the early numbness starts to wear off and you begin to be confronted with the reality of the death.

This dimension of grief may give rise to what I sometimes call "going-crazy syndrome." Mourners often say, "I think I'm going crazy." That's because in grief, thoughts and behaviors are different from what you normally experience. If you feel disorganized and confused, know that you are not going crazy, you are grieving. (For more on going-crazy syndrome, see Touchstone Six.)

You may feel a sense of restlessness, agitation, impatience, and ongoing confusion. It's like being in the middle of a wild, rushing river where you can't get a grasp on anything. Disconnected thoughts race through your mind, and strong, jumbled emotions may be overwhelming.

You may notice your disorganization and confusion in your inability to complete tasks. You may start to do something but never finish it.

You may feel forgetful and ineffective, especially early in the morning and late at night, when fatigue and lethargy are most prominent.

You might also experience a conscious or subconscious searching for the person who has died. You might even feel a shift in perception; other people may begin to look like the person who died. You might be at a store, look down an aisle, and think you glimpse the person you love so much. Or you might see a familiar car whiz past and find yourself following it in hopes that the person who died is somehow inside. For a period of months (or even much longer), your mind may continue to look for the person—in your home, in crowds, in places that they used to frequent. You may expect them to phone you or to walk through the door at any moment. This happens because it simply takes time for our minds and hearts to fully understand and acknowledge the reality and finality of a death.

> *"It doesn't seem worth starting anything. I can't settle down."*
>
> C.S. Lewis

Visual hallucinations occur so frequently in grief that they can't be considered abnormal. I personally prefer the term "memory picture" to hallucination. As part of your searching and yearning, you may not only catch fleeting glimpses of the person who died, you may also experience a sense of their presence.

What's more, you may dream about the person who died. Dreams can be an unconscious means of searching for them. Be careful not to overinterpret your dreams. Simply remain open to pondering their mystery. If the dreams are pleasant, embrace them; if they're disturbing, talk about them with someone who'll empathize without judgment or advice-giving.

Yearning, too, is normal. This is the intense, near-constant ache of missing the person who died. They're gone, and you want them back. Yearning and preoccupation with memories can leave you feeling drained.

Other common experiences that often go hand-in-hand with disorganization, confusion, searching, and yearning are difficulties with eating and sleeping. You may experience a loss of appetite or find yourself overeating. Even when you do eat, you may be unable to taste the food. Having trouble falling asleep and early morning awakening are also common experiences associated with this dimension of grief.

"My heart and body are crying out, come back, come back."

C.S. Lewis

And finally, keep in mind that disorganization after a loss always comes before any kind of reorganization. While they may seem strange, feelings of disorganization, confusion, searching, and yearning are actually steppingstones on your path toward reconciliation.

SELF-CARE GUIDELINES

If disorganization, confusion, searching, and yearning are, or have been, a part of your grief journey, don't worry about the normalcy of your experience. A critically important point is to never forget these reassuring words: You are not crazy!

The thoughts, feelings, and behaviors of this dimension don't come all at once. They are often experienced in a wavelike fashion. You may need to talk and cry for long periods of time. At other times, you may just need to be alone. Don't try to interpret what you think and feel. Just think and feel it. Sometimes when you talk, you may feel you're not making much sense. And you may not be. But nonetheless, talking out your confusion can still be self-clarifying, even if at a subconscious level.

When you feel disoriented, tell someone who will understand. To integrate loss into your life, grief must be shared outside of yourself. I hope you have at least one person whom you feel understands and will not judge you. That person must be patient and attentive because you may need to talk through confusing thoughts and feelings over and over again as you work to integrate your grief. They must be genuinely interested in understanding you. If you are trying to express your disorganization and confusion but the person with whom you're speaking doesn't want to listen, find someone else who will better meet your needs.

When you're feeling disorganized or confused, avoid making any critical, major decisions, like selling your house or quitting your job. Your judgment may not be the best right now, and ill-timed decisions can result in more losses. Go slow and be patient with yourself.

EXPRESS YOURSELF:
Go to your *Understanding Your Grief Journal* on pp. 90-92.

Anxiety, Panic, and Fear

Feelings of anxiety, panic, and fear are also very typical in grief. You might be asking yourself, "Am I going to be OK? Will I survive this? Will my life have any purpose without this person?" These kinds of

---

THOUGHTS ON RESILIENCE

Resilience is often defined as the capacity to bounce back after difficult life losses and transitions. When you're grieving, it's a concept to be aware of and watch out for.

In our mourning-avoidant culture, people sometimes put resilience on a pedestal. They may mistakenly equate it with being strong in grief and "getting over it" quickly. But that's not resilience—that's denial.

True resilience in grief doesn't mean being phony or avoiding your grief. Instead, it means intentionally choosing actions known to support healing. It means embracing the realities of grief. It means befriending and expressing all the feelings we're reviewing in this chapter. It means authentically sharing them with others. It means cultivating connection and hope.

Resilience is a skill that can be practiced and learned. Whenever you choose to think and act with authenticity, compassion, hope, and gratitude—toward yourself and others—you are cultivating true resilience.

questions are natural. Your sense of security has been threatened, so you are naturally anxious.

A variety of thoughts and situations can increase your anxiety, panic, and fear. For example, you may be afraid of what the future holds or that other people in your life could die soon. You may be more aware of your own mortality, which can be scary. You may feel vulnerable, even unable to survive, without the person who died. You may feel panicky about your inability to concentrate. Financial problems can compound feelings of anxiety.

Your sleep might be affected by fear at this time, too. Fears of overwhelming, painful thoughts and feelings that can come up in dreams may cause you difficulty with sleeping. Or you may be afraid of being alone in your house. Again, these are normal, but usually temporary, ways that fear can be part of your grief.

"No one ever told me grief felt so much like fear."

C.S. Lewis

Anxiety sometimes shows up in the form of **panic attacks**. Panic is a sudden, overpowering feeling of terror, often accompanied by physical symptoms such as a racing heart, sweating, chest pain, nausea, and more. People sometimes feel like they're dying when they experience a panic attack. Panic attacks usually only last for a few minutes, but they are often terrifying. I have seen numerous grieving people in counseling whose panic attacks were the doorway to get them to give attention to their grief and learn to authentically mourn.

While unpleasant, anxiety, panic, and fear are often normal components of grief. The good news is that expressing them usually makes them more tolerable. And knowing that they are temporary may also help you during these trying experiences.

SELF-CARE GUIDELINES
If anxiety, panic, and fear are a part of your grief journey, you will need to talk about them with someone who will be understanding

and supportive. Conversely, not talking about these feelings makes them so much more powerful and destructive.

You will find it helpful to talk about your fears and anxieties. If you don't talk about them, you may find yourself retreating from other people and from the world in general. I have seen many grieving people become prisoners in their own homes. They repress their anxiety, panic, and fear, only to discover that these feelings are now repressing them. I encourage you to not allow your fears and anxieties to go unexpressed.

And if you are experiencing panic attacks, be sure to seek help from your primary-care provider or a grief counselor. They are simply a sign that you need some extra support.

EXPRESS YOURSELF:
Go to your *Understanding Your Grief Journal* on pp. 92-93.

Explosive Emotions

Anger, hate, blame, terror, resentment, rage, and jealousy are explosive emotions that may be a volatile yet natural part of your grief journey. It helps to understand that all of these feelings are, at bottom, a form of protest. Think of the toddler whose favorite toy is yanked out of his hands. This toddler wants the toy; when it's taken, his instinctive reaction is to scream or cry or hit. When someone loved is taken from you, your instinctive reaction may be much the same.

Explosive emotions can surface at any time after someone you love has died. You might cry out in anguish, "How could this happen? This isn't fair! I hate this!" You may find yourself directing your anger at the person who died, at friends and family members, at doctors, at people who haven't experienced loss, at God, or even at yourself.

Unfortunately, our culture doesn't understand how normal and necessary explosive emotions can be. Expressing volatile emotions is typically judged as wrong. The implicit message is that you should try to "keep it together." When you're raging or terrified, others may get upset. You may even get upset by the intensity of your own emotions. Still, you must give yourself permission to feel whatever you feel and to express those feelings. If you collaborate with the well-intentioned but misinformed people who encourage you to repress strong emotions, your body, mind, and spirit will probably be damaged in the process.

> *"Why is He (God) so present a commander in our time of prosperity and so very absent a help in time of trouble?"*
>
> C.S. Lewis

Some people may tell you that explosive emotions aren't logical. "Anger won't bring him back," they might say. "He didn't mean to die, so don't be mad at him." Watch out. You might find yourself buying into this rational thinking. That's just the problem—thinking is logical; feeling is not.

Another problem is that people oversimplify explosive emotions by talking only about anger. Actually, you may experience a whole range of intense feelings such as those previously mentioned: anger, hate, blame, terror, resentment, rage, and jealousy. Underneath all of these protest emotions are usually feelings of pain, helplessness, fear, and hurt.

If explosive emotions are part of your journey (and they aren't for everyone), be aware that you have two avenues for expression—outward or inward. The outward avenue leads to healing; the inward avenue does not. Keeping your explosive emotions inside can cause low self-esteem, depression, guilt, physical complaints, and sometimes even persistent thoughts of suicide. (Please see p. 89 for more on suicidal thoughts and feelings.)

Explosive emotions are normal. They should, however, moderate in intensity and duration as you do the work of mourning. Again, I want to emphasize that the key is finding someone who will allow you to express any explosive emotions without inhibition or judgment, as long as you are not hurting yourself or anyone else, physically or emotionally. **Remember—you can't go around your**

grief or over it or under it—you must go through it. I hope that
as you journey through grief you will be surrounded by people who
understand, support, and love you and will help you explore your
explosive emotions without trying to stifle you.

SELF-CARE GUIDELINES
Explosive emotions must be expressed, not repressed or, worse yet,
totally denied. Don't expect or force yourself to have these feelings,
but do be on the alert for them if they naturally arise. You will need
a supportive listener who can tolerate, encourage, and validate your
explosive emotions without judging, retaliating, or arguing with you.
The comforting presence of someone who cares about you will help
you seek self-understanding.

Be aware, though, of the difference between the right to feel
explosive emotions and the right to act out these emotions in
harmful ways. It's OK, sometimes even necessary, to feel angry. But
if you hurt others or yourself or destroy property, the people who
care about you will rightfully need to set limits on your behavior.
Also, remind yourself that explosive emotions are usually masking
underlying feelings of pain, helplessness, frustration, fear, and hurt.
Befriend your explosive emotions and discover and embrace what's
beneath them.

As you journey through your grief, continue to remind yourself that
explosive emotions are not good or bad, right or wrong. They just
are. They are your feelings, and they are symptoms of an injury that
needs nurturing, not judging. Paradoxically, the way to diminish
explosive emotions is to experience and express them, even when
they feel irrational or overwhelming to you.

EXPRESS YOURSELF:
Go to your *Understanding Your Grief Journal* on pp. 94-95.

Guilt and Regret
Guilt, regret, and self-blame are common and natural feelings after
the death of someone loved. You may have a case of the "if-onlys": If

only I had gotten him to the doctor sooner… If only I had been with her that night… If only I hadn't said…

If you find yourself experiencing such regrets, please be compassionate with yourself. When someone you care about dies, it's normal to think about actions you could or could not have taken before the death, whether to prevent it, to have done everything you could, or simply to have closed the loop on any unfinished business. But of course, human lives are not so neat. It's simply impossible to go through life in close relationships with other people without saying or doing something you later wish you could change—or not saying or not doing something you later wish you had.

While these feelings of guilt and regret are natural, they are sometimes not logical to those around you. When you express them, some people may say, "Don't be silly. There was nothing you could have done." Whether you could have done something or not is beside the point. The point is that you are *feeling like* you could have or should have, and you need to express those feelings, however illogical they may be.

Other aspects of guilt and regret after a death may include:

SURVIVOR GUILT

Sometimes being alive after someone you love has died causes what's termed "survivor guilt." Have you found yourself thinking, "Why did they die and not me?" This is a natural question. It may be a part of your grief experience. If it is, find someone who will be understanding and allow you to talk it out.

RELIEF-GUILT

If someone you love dies after a long period of illness and suffering, you may naturally feel some relief. But your feelings of relief can also make you feel guilty. "I shouldn't be feeling relieved," you may think.

Relief-guilt may also arise when you recognize that you won't miss certain aspects of the relationship you had with the person who died. For example, you probably wouldn't miss how the person belittled you or any behavior that caused family distress. Or, to give a milder example, you likely wouldn't miss being late to appointments because the person who died was always running behind schedule.

To *not* miss some things about the person who died is fine. This doesn't mean you didn't love the person. An understanding listener can help you explore this as part of your work of mourning.

JOY-GUILT

Like relief-guilt, joy-guilt is about thinking that lighter, happier feelings are wrong at a time of loss. Experiencing any kind of joy after the death makes some people feel guilty. One day you might find yourself smiling or laughing at something, only to chastise yourself for having felt happy for a minute. It's as if your loyalty to the person who died demands that you be sad all the time now that they're gone. That's not true, of course. As you do the work of mourning, your natural healing journey will allow to start experiencing more and more joy and less and less pain. If you find yourself feeling guilty about the joy, find someone to talk to about it.

MAGICAL THINKING AND GUILT

Consciously or unconsciously wishing for the death of someone loved—and then having that "wish" come true—can make you feel guilty. We call this magical thinking, because, of course, your thoughts didn't cause the death.

At some point in your relationship, you may have thought, "I wish you would go away and leave me alone." Or, if the relationship was extremely difficult, you may even have had more direct thoughts about death ending the relationship. If so, you may now feel somehow responsible for the death. Know that all relationships have periods in which negative thoughts prevail. But even so, your mind doesn't have the power to inflict death. If you are struggling with any such thoughts, find someone to talk with who will be understanding and nonjudgmental.

LONGSTANDING PERSONALITY FACTORS

Some people have felt guilty their entire lives. I hope you're not one of them, but you may be. Why? Because some people are taught early in life, typically during childhood, that they are responsible when something bad happens. When someone dies, it's just one more thing to feel guilty about. If all-encompassing guilt is part of your experience, seek out a professional counselor who can help you work on understanding the nature and extent of any deep-seated guilt.

> *"Still, there's no denying that in some sense I 'feel better,' and with that comes at once a sort of shame, and a feeling that one is under a sort of obligation to cherish and foment and prolong one's unhappiness."*
>
> C.S. Lewis

Whatever your unique feelings of guilt and regret may be, don't let them go unexpressed. They are a natural part of your journey, and like all dimensions of grief, they need to be explored. So don't try to make this journey alone! Find a compassionate friend who will walk with you and listen to you without judgment.

And I would be remiss if I did not note here that occasionally mourners are in fact partly or wholly responsible for the death of someone loved. If your accidental or intentional actions contributed to the death, please seek help from an experienced, well-trained grief counselor. Your feelings of guilt and remorse will certainly complicate your grief journey, and you will need assistance effectively engaging with these sometimes all-consuming feelings.

SELF-CARE GUIDELINES

If any aspect of guilt and regret are a part of your grief experience, look for a compassionate, patient, and nonjudgmental listener. If you feel it, acknowledge it and express it openly.

Don't allow others to dismiss or explain your feelings away. While they may be trying to help you, this attitude will not allow you to talk out what you think and feel on the inside. As you openly and honestly explore any feelings of guilt and regret, you will come to understand the limits of your own responsibility.

As you express yourself, remember—you aren't perfect. None of us are. Something happened that you wish had not. Someone you care about died. Now you will naturally go back and review if you could have said or done anything to change this difficult reality. Allow yourself this review time, but as you do so, be compassionate with yourself. Continue to remind yourself that there are many things in life that people cannot control or change.

One of the worst things you could do is ignore or repress feelings of guilt. Many physical and emotional problems will result if you try to suppress or push these feelings away without talking them out. And if you feel stuck on emotions of guilt or regret, don't be ashamed to find a compassionate grief counselor.

EXPRESS YOURSELF:
Go to your *Understanding Your Grief Journal* on pp. 96-97.

Sadness and Depression

Sadness can be the most hurtful feeling on your journey through grief. We don't want to be sad. Sadness saps pleasure from our lives. Sadness makes us feel bad.

> "*The act of living is different all through. Her absence is like the sky, spread all over everything.*"
>
> C.S. Lewis

But sadness is a natural, authentic emotion after the death of someone loved. Something precious in your life is now gone. Of course you are sad. Of course you feel deep sorrow. Allowing yourself to feel your sadness is in large part what your journey toward healing is all about. I suggest you say out loud right now, "I have every right to feel sad!"

I would even argue that it's necessary to feel sad and depressed. But *why* is it necessary? Why does the emotion we call sadness have to exist at all? Couldn't we just move from loss to shock to reconciliation without all that pain in the middle?

The answer is that depression plays an essential role. It forces us to regroup—physically, cognitively, emotionally, socially, and spiritually. When we are sad, we instinctively turn inward. We withdraw. We slow down. It's as if our soul presses the pause button and says,

THE DARK NIGHT OF THE SOUL

While grief affects all aspects of your life—your physical, cognitive, emotional, social, and spiritual selves—it is fundamentally a spiritual journey.

In grief, your understanding of who you are, why you are here, and whether or not life is worth living is challenged. A significant loss plunges you into what C.S. Lewis, Eckhart Tolle, and various Christian mystics have called "the dark night of the soul." Life may suddenly seem meaningless. Nothing makes sense. Everything you believed and held dear may have been turned upside-down. The structure of your world might seem to have collapsed.

The dark night of the soul can be a long and very black night indeed. It is uncomfortable and scary. The pain of that place can seem intolerable, and yet the only way to emerge into the light of a new morning is to experience the night.

I often note that **one of the main paradoxes of grief is that you must make friends with the darkness before you can enter the light**. The natural sadness and depression of your grief live in that darkness. Be present to them in doses. Sit with them, get to know them, and express them outside of yourself. The more you allow yourself to feel and attend to your natural sadness, the more momentum you will gain on your journey toward healing.

"Whoa, whoa, whoaaa. Time out. I need to acknowledge what's happened here and really consider what I want to do next."

The natural depression of grief slows down your body and prevents major organ systems from being damaged. It aids in your healing and provides time to slowly begin re-ordering your life. These natural feelings can ultimately help you explore where you are, assess old ways of being, and make plans for the future.

I sometimes call the necessary sadness of grief "sitting in your wound." When you sit in the wound of your grief, you surrender to it. You acquiesce to the instinct to slow down and turn inward. You allow yourself to appropriately be with and feel the pain. You shut the world out for a time so that, eventually, you have created space to let the world back in.

Weeks, or often months, will pass before you are fully confronted by the depth of your sorrow. The slowly growing nature of this awareness is good. You could not and should not try to tolerate all of your sadness at once. Your body, mind, and spirit need time working together to embrace the depth of your loss. Be patient with yourself. Surround yourself with loving people who will understand you, not judge you.

You may find that certain times and circumstances make you feel sadder than others. Grieving people often tell me that weekends, holidays, family meals, and any kind of anniversary occasion can be hard. So can bedtime, waking up in the morning, awakening in the middle of the night, and arriving home to an empty house. Difficult times often have some kind of connection to the person who died.

Unfortunately, our culture has an unwritten rule that says while physical illness is usually beyond our control, emotional distress is our fault. In other words, some people think you should be able to control or subdue your feelings of sadness.

Nothing could be further from the truth. Your sadness is a normal symptom of your wound. Just as physical wounds require attention, so do emotional wounds.

NORMAL GRIEF OR CLINICAL DEPRESSION?

For centuries, most people viewed depression as a sign of physical or mental weakness, not as a real health problem. But today, clinical depression is recognized as a common health challenge—an illness with a biological basis that is often exacerbated by psychological and social stress. In fact, each year about ten percent of American adults experience some form of clinical depression.

There are a number of influences that can play a role in the development of depression, including genetics, stress (such as the death of someone you love), and changes in body and brain function. Many people with clinical depression have abnormally low levels of certain brain chemicals and slowed cellular activity in areas of the brain that control mood, appetite, sleep, and other functions.

Clinical depression affects not only your mood but also how you think about things, making your thoughts more negative and pessimistic. It affects how you feel about yourself, lowering your sense of self-worth. It impacts how you act, often making you more ambivalent or disinterested in life and can make you easily upset about even minor things.

Everyone experiences times of sadness in response to the stresses and losses of life. The feelings that go along with these stressful events are naturally unpleasant. Yet the occasional sadness that we all sometimes feel because of life's disappointments and stresses is very different from clinical depression. Unlike normal feelings of sadness and loss, clinical depression can be debilitating.

In many ways, depression and grief are similar. Common shared symptoms are feelings of sadness, lack of interest in usually pleasurable activities, and problems with eating and sleeping. The central difference is that while grief is a normal, natural, and healthy process, clinical depression is not.

One area to pay particular attention to is feelings of self-worth. While people who are grieving a death often feel guilty over some aspect of the relationship or the circumstances of the death, they do not typically feel worthless. In other words, people with grief depression may feel guilty and even hopeless for a time, while people with clinical depression often feel a generalized sense of low self-worth and hopelessness.

NORMAL GRIEF	CLINICAL DEPRESSION
You have normal grief if you...	You may be clinically depressed if you...
○ respond to comfort and support.	○ do not accept support.
○ are capable of being openly angry.	○ are irritable and complain but do not directly express anger.
○ relate your depressed feelings to the loss experience.	○ do not relate your feelings of depression to a particular life event.
○ can still experience moments of enjoyment in life.	○ exhibit an all-pervading sense of gloom.
○ exhibit feelings of sadness and emptiness.	○ project a sense of hopelessness and chronic emptiness.
○ may have transient physical complaints.	○ have chronic physical complaints.
○ express guilt over some specific aspect of the loss.	○ have generalized feelings of guilt.
○ feel a temporary loss of self-esteem.	○ feel a deep and ongoing loss of self-esteem.

The difference between the normal sadness of grief and clinical depression can also be measured by how long the feelings last and to what extent your daily activities are impaired. Grief softens over time; clinical depression does not. After the numbing and chaotic early days and weeks of grief, your daily schedule begins to proceed as usual. If you are clinically depressed, you may be unable to function day-to-day.

Depression can complicate grief in two ways. It can create short-term symptoms that are more severe and debilitating than those normally associated with grief. In addition, clinical depression can cause symptoms of grief to persist longer than normal and potentially worsen. (Continued on next page.)

If you or someone who cares about you thinks you may be clinically depressed, I invite you to review the chart on the previous page and make a checkmark next to any symptoms you think apply to you. If you place checkmarks in the clinical depression column, that means it's time to see your primary-care provider or a counselor. They will help you discern what's going on and get you the extra care you need. Remember—getting help is not a sign of weakness; it is a sign of strength.

The good news is that clinical depression is treatable. With appropriate assessment and treatment, most people with clinical depression find significant relief. Untreated depression, on the other hand, can raise your risk for a number of additional health problems. It will also prevent you from moving forward in your journey through grief. You deserve to get help so you can continue to mourn in ways that help you heal. Choose life!

Paradoxically, **the only way to lessen your pain is to move toward it, not away from it**. Yet I realize that moving toward your sadness is not easy to do. Every time you admit to feeling sad, some people around you may say things like, "Oh, don't be sad" or "Get a hold of yourself" or "Just think about what you have to be thankful for." Comments like these hinder, not help, your healing.

For some grievers, the normal depression of grief can become debilitating enough to be classified as clinical depression. After all, grief and mourning share many symptoms with depression, including sleep disturbances, appetite changes, decreased energy, withdrawal, guilt, dependency, lack of concentration, and a sense of loss of control. You may be having a hard time functioning at home and at work, which may compound your feelings of isolation and helplessness. If you feel totally immobilized, please get help from understanding friends or a professional counselor. If you're unsure if you're experiencing normal grief or clinical depression, seek out help.

Thoughts of suicide may also occur during your grief journey. Hundreds of grieving people have shared with me thoughts like, "I wouldn't mind if I didn't wake up tomorrow." When someone you love dies, it's natural to experience these passive and passing thoughts about dying; it's not natural to want to, or make plans to, take your own life.

If you've been thinking of taking your own life, talk to a professional helper immediately. Today! Suicidal thoughts are sometimes an expression of wanting to find relief from the pain of grief. Yes, you have been injured and you hurt. But to help your injury heal, you must talk openly about what this death has meant for you.

SELF-CARE GUIDELINES

As you embrace your feelings of sadness, you will need the comfort of trusted people—close friends, loving family members, and sometimes compassionate professional helpers. Your natural feelings of sadness can leave you feeling isolated and alone. Consequently, you will need to talk them out with accepting and understanding people. Talk to them about the death and its meaning to you. You need people to validate what you feel. You need people who will sometimes walk with you—not behind or in front of you but beside you—on your path through the wilderness.

Keep talking until you have exhausted your capacity to talk. Doing so will help reconnect you with the world outside of yourself. Or if you can't talk it out, write it out! Paint it out! Sing it out! Do anything you want—just get the feelings outside of yourself. And give yourself permission to cry—as often and as much as you need to. Tears can help you cleanse your body, mind, and spirit.

Most important is to remember that temporary feelings of sadness and depression have value in your grief journey. As long as they are not clinical depression, they are not destructive but rather constructive feelings. They cause you to slow down and give your grief the time and attention it needs, which in turn allows you to begin to explore and discover meaning in the life of the person who died and their relationship with you. These feelings also give you the space you need to reconstruct your own self-identity and rebuild meaning and purpose in your life moving forward.

EXPRESS YOURSELF:
Go to your *Understanding Your Grief Journal* on pp. 98-100.

Relief and Release

As noted under the section on guilt and regret, sometimes you may feel a sense of relief and release when someone you love dies, such as when a death follows a long, dificult illness. Any relief you feel, then, is normal and natural, and it does not equate to a lack of love for the person who died.

When you anticipate the death of someone who is terminally ill, you begin grieving and, I hope, mourning, long before the death itself.

> *"Something quite unexpected has happened...my heart is lighter than it has been for weeks."*
>
> C.S. Lewis

Your grief journey actually begins when the person you love enters the transition from living to dying. When you watch someone you love endure physical pain and loss of quality of life, you begin to understand that death can bring relief. And so when the death occurs, your feelings of relief may be just as pronounced as your other feelings.

Another form of relief you may experience comes when you finally express your thoughts and feelings about a death. If you have largely repressed or denied these feelings up until now, when you do express them you may feel as if a great pressure has been lifted from your head, heart, and soul.

Allowing yourself to acknowledge relief as a part of your grief experience can be a critical step in your journey. Working to embrace these feelings creates the opportunity to find hope in your healing.

SELF-CARE GUIDELINES
If you feel a sense of relief or release, write about it, or better yet, talk it out. Again, find someone you trust who will listen and hear you. If you feel guilty about being relieved, talk about it with someone who can help you feel understood. Whatever you do, don't isolate yourself. Share your feelings!

EXPRESS YOURSELF:
Go to your *Understanding Your Grief Journal* on p. 101.

A Final Thought about the Feelings You May Experience

When you add up all the thoughts and feelings you've had since the death of the person you love—as well as all the emotions you're yet to have in the months to come—we call this experience "grief." It's a deceptively small, simple word for such a wide-ranging, challenging assortment of feelings.

The ways you behave when you're having these feelings is also part of your grief journey. Mourning—or expressing your feelings outside of yourself—is sometimes, but not always, intentional. Your feelings may come out in strange and unpredictable ways, and this, too, is normal.

I hope you will be kind to yourself as you encounter and befriend all your grief feelings and behaviors. Patience is paramount, as is self-compassion. You feel what you feel; there are no rights or wrongs. And when you're struggling with your feelings or need to let them out, I hope you'll remember to reach out to the people who care about you. Having the feelings is normal and necessary, but so is expressing them outside of yourself and having them affirmed by others.

This is the cycle of experiencing a feeling in grief: feel it, acknowledge it, befriend it, share it, and finally, have it witnessed

and empathized with by others. Repeat. Each time you complete the circle, you are taking one small step toward integrating this loss into your life.

EXPRESS YOURSELF:
Go to *The Understanding Your Grief Journal* on pp. 102.

Understand the
Six Needs of Mourning

If you are hoping for a map for your journey through grief, none exists. Your wilderness is an undiscovered wilderness and you its first explorer.

"Life seems sometimes like nothing more than a series of losses, from beginning to end. That's the given. How you respond to those losses, what you make of what's left, that's the part you have to make up as you go."

Katharine Weber

Yet virtually all mourners who have journeyed before you have found that their paths are similar. In grief, there are more commonalities than there are differences. In an effort to describe these similarities, a number of authors have described models of grief that refer to "stages." But as I suggested in Touchstone Two about grief misconceptions, we do not go through orderly, predictable, and sequential stages of grief with clear-cut beginnings and endings.

Still, when we are in mourning, we do share the same basic needs. Instead of referring to stages of grief, I say that we as mourners have six central needs. Remember I said in the Introduction that as we journey through grief, we need to follow the trail markers, or the touchstones, if we are to find our way out of the wilderness? The trail marker we will discuss in this chapter defines the six central needs of mourning. You might think of Touchstone Five as its own little grouping of trail markers.

The six needs of mourning aren't orderly or predictable. Though I've numbered them for easy reference, they aren't really sequential. You will probably jump around in random fashion as you work on these six needs of mourning. You will address each need when you are ready to do so. And sometimes you will be working on more than one need at a time.

You will find that several of the six needs of mourning reiterate and reinforce concepts found in other chapters of this book, such as opening to the reality and pain of the loss. I hope this reinforcement helps you embrace how very important these fundamental concepts are.

What's more, **your awareness of these needs will help you take a participative, action-oriented approach to healing in grief as opposed to thinking of grief as something you passively experience.** You'll recall in Touchstone Two that we reviewed the important distinction between grief and mourning. Grief is what you think and feel on the inside; mourning is when you express those thoughts and feelings outside of yourself. These are not called the six needs of grief but rather the six needs of mourning. Why? Because while you will naturally experience all of them internally, to integrate them into your life, you will also need to intentionally, proactively engage with all of them externally as well.

Grief is the noun; mourning is the verb.

Grief is the vehicle; mourning is the engine.

Grief is the rock; mourning is the catapult.

THE SIX NEEDS OF MOURNING

1. Acknowledge the reality of the death.

2. Embrace the pain of the loss.

3. Remember the person who died.

4. Develop a new self-identity.

5. Search for meaning.

6. Let others help you— now and always.

The magic of the six needs of mourning is that while they're painful and difficult, they're also, over time, transformative. They will carry you through the wilderness of your grief. They'll help give you the momentum you need to not only survive but eventually thrive again.

MOURNING NEED 1:

Acknowledge the Reality of the Death

You can know something in your head but not in your heart. This is often what happens in the early days and weeks after someone you love dies. This first need of mourning, a close cousin to Touchstone One (Open to the Presence of Your Loss), involves gently confronting the reality that someone you care about will never physically be present in your life again.

Whether the death was sudden or anticipated, acknowledging the full reality of the loss will unfold slowly, over the course of weeks and months. You may expect the person who died to come through the door, to call on the phone, or even to touch you. To survive, you may try to push away the reality of the death at times. This is normal. Accepting the painful reality that someone you love has died is not quick, easy, or efficient. It's normal to move back and forth between evading and encountering the reality. In fact, encountering the reality is such a difficult task that it can only be accomplished a little bit at a time, in small doses.

> *"Acknowledgment of grief—well, it makes feeling the grief easier, not harder."*
>
> Elizabeth McCracken

You may also discover yourself replaying moments—good and bad—leading up to and including the time of the death. This replay is a vital, normal part of this need of mourning. It's as if each time you think and talk it out, the death becomes a little more real.

As you continue to encounter the reality of the death, your feelings about it may fluctuate. One moment the reality may seem tolerable; another moment it may feel unbearable. Be patient with this need. At times you might feel like running away and hiding. At other times you may hope you will awaken from what seems like a bad dream.

In the early months, your thoughts and feelings will naturally turn toward the death on most days. Don't forget to share them outside yourself as well. Talk to compassionate friends about these thoughts and feelings. Write about them in the *Understanding Your Grief Journal*. Consider joining a support group or online forum when you're ready. Find ways to move your internal struggle with the reality of the death from the inside to the outside.

Remember—this first need of mourning, like the other five that follow—may intermittently require your attention for months and even years. Be patient and compassionate with yourself as you work on each of them.

EXPRESS YOURSELF:
Go to *The Understanding Your Grief Journal* on pp. 104-105.

MOURNING NEED 2:
Embrace the Pain of the Loss

Like Touchstone One: Open to the Presence of Your Loss, this need of mourning requires us to embrace the pain of our grief—something we naturally don't want to do. After all, it's easier to avoid, repress, or deny the pain of grief than it is to greet it head-on, yet it is in confronting our pain that we learn to reconcile ourselves to it.

In the grief-caregiver training courses I teach, my students often ask me what I mean by "embracing" the pain of grief. I also like to use the verb "befriending," and people ask about that term as well. When I say that this need of mourning is to embrace your pain, I'm first asking you to acknowledge the appropriateness of the pain. Someone you love—someone who gave your life meaning—has died. Of course it hurts! Of course you feel pain! Where there was love or attachment, there will naturally be pain when a relationship is severed by death.

But in addition to emphasizing that you must recognize your pain as normal, I'm further suggesting that over time you even need to learn to look upon your pain as part of your love and make it your friend. As you probably realize, love and grief are two sides of the same

> "I miss her all the time. The only difference is that I am getting used to the pain."
>
> Rachel Joyce

precious coin. If your love is good and valuable, so, too, is your grief. And like your love, it will require your loving attention in the months and years to come.

Even so, you will discover that you need to dose yourself in embracing your pain. We've discussed this already, but here's a reminder: you cannot (nor should you try to) overload yourself with the hurt all at one time. Sometimes you may need to distract yourself from the pain of your grief, while at other times you will need to create a safe place to move toward it.

What's more, feeling your pain can sometimes zap you of your energy. When your energy is low, you may be tempted to suppress your grief or even run from it. If you start running and keep running, you may never heal. Dose your pain: yes! Deny your pain: no!

Unfortunately, as I have said, our culture tends to encourage the denial of pain. We misunderstand the role of suffering. If you openly express your feelings of grief, misinformed friends may advise you to "carry on" or "keep your chin up." If, on the other hand, you remain "strong" and "in control," you may be congratulated for "doing well" with your grief. Actually, doing well with your grief means becoming well acquainted with your pain. Don't let others deny you this critical mourning need.

And of course, embracing the pain of grief is also an active mourning process. You will befriend your pain by sitting with it, being present to it, and thinking about and feeling it. But to convert grief into mourning, you must also express it outside of yourself regularly. Cry if you feel like crying, and let your tears be seen and heard by people who care about you. Tell your friends and family what you are thinking and feeling. Describe your pain to them. People who listen without judging are your most important helpers as you work on this mourning need. As you encounter your pain, you will also need to nurture yourself in all the ways we will discuss in Touchstone Seven.

Never forget that grief requires convalescence: something that by its nature is slow and recursive. Your pain will probably ebb and flow for months, even years; embracing it when it washes it over you will require patience, support, and strength.

EXPRESS YOURSELF:
Go to *The Understanding Your Grief Journal* on pp. 106-107.

MOURNING NEED 3:

Remember the Person Who Died

Do you have any kind of relationship with someone after they die? Of course. You have a relationship of memory. Precious memories, dreams reflecting the significance of the relationship, and objects that link you to the person who died (such as photos, souvenirs, clothing, etc.) are examples of some of the things that give testimony to a different form of a continued relationship. This need of mourning involves allowing and encouraging yourself to pursue this relationship.

> *"Memories are the key not to the past but to the future."*
>
> Corrie ten Boom

The process of beginning to embrace your memories often begins with the funeral. The ritual offers you an opportunity to remember the person who died and helps affirm the value of the life that was lived. The memories you embrace during the time of the funeral set the tone for the changed nature of the relationship. And later on, additional meaningful rituals (see p. 105) encourage the expression of cherished memories and allow for both tears and laughter in the company of others who loved the person who died.

Embracing your memories can be a very slow and, at times, painful process that occurs in small steps. Remember—don't try to do all of your work of mourning at once. Go slowly and be patient with yourself.

But some people may try to take your memories away. Trying to be helpful, they may encourage you to take down all the photos of the person who died, for example. They might tell you to keep busy or even to move out of your house. You, too, may think avoiding memories would be better for you. And why not? You are living in a culture that teaches you that to move away from your grief—instead of toward it—is best.

Don't believe it. Actively and intentionally remember instead.

Following are a few examples of things you can do to keep memories

ON GOING BACKWARD BEFORE YOU CAN GO FORWARD

Our culture may be encouraging you to move on, but one of the paradoxes of grief is that you have to go backward before you can go forward.

Grief by its very nature is a recursive process. That means it curves and spirals back on itself. It's repetitive. It covers the same ground more than once. Lots of times it's not even a two-steps-forward, one-step-backward kind of journey. Instead, it's often a one-step-forward, two-steps-in-a-circle, one-step-backward process. It takes time, patience, and yes, lots of backward motion before forward motion predominates.

When you actively remember the person who died, you go backward. When you tell the story of your love and loss from the beginning, you go backward. When you think back to earlier losses in your life and how they may be affecting your current grief, you go backward. When you work on your self-identity and think back to old interests you may now want to revisit, you go backward. These and other backward-looking activities are a normal and necessary part of grief.

So by all means, go backward as much and as often as you need to. As long as you are actively engaging with your grief, you can trust that one day you will look up and find that you have indeed moved forward in meaningful ways.

alive while at the same time acknowledging the reality of the death:

- Talking out or writing out favorite memories
- Giving yourself permission to keep special keepsakes or "linking objects" (see p. 119)
- Displaying photos of the person who died
- Visiting places of special significance that stimulate memories of times shared together
- Reviewing photo albums at special times such as holidays, birthdays, and anniversaries

Perhaps one of the best ways to embrace memories is by creating a memory book that contains special photographs you've selected and perhaps other memorabilia, such as ticket stubs, menus, etc. Organize these items, place them in a physical album or create one online, and write out the memories reflected in the photos. This book can then become a valued collection of memories you can review whenever you want.

The act of creating a memory book is mourning. Showing it to others and talking about it is, too. Of course, you don't need a memory book to mourn your memories. You can simply sit down with a friend and talk about them, or you can post photos online and write a little about what they mean to you.

I also need to mention here the reality that memories are not always pleasant. If this applies to you, addressing this need of mourning can be even more difficult, but to ignore painful or ambivalent memories is to prevent yourself from living fully for the rest of your life. You will need someone who can nonjudgmentally explore any painful memories with you. If you repress or deny these memories, you risk carrying an underlying sadness or anger into your future. If your memories are particularly challenging or traumatic, I urge you to see a counselor who is trained to help you with memory work.

When people share their fond memories of the person who died with you, this can be a great gift. Welcome and cherish these new stories, and add them to your storehouse of treasures. Yet I also know that sometimes others may share memories and information with you that are not so pleasant. Many mourners have told me that only after a death did they learn surprising or disturbing secrets about someone who died. These revelations can be exceptionally hard to integrate into your understanding of the person's life, especially since the person is no longer here to discuss them with. If this happens to you and you are having trouble coming to terms with new information, I urge you to see a counselor for a few sessions. A skilled, compassionate professional will be able to help you through this understandably confusing time.

In general, however, **remembering the past makes hoping for the future possible**. Your future will become open to new experiences only to the extent that you embrace the past.

EXPRESS YOURSELF:
Go to *The Understanding Your Grief Journal* on pp. 108-115.

MOURNING NEED 4:
Develop a New Self-Identity

Your personal identity, or self-perception, is the result of the ongoing process of establishing a sense of who you are. Part of your self-identity comes from the relationships you have with other people. When someone with whom you have a relationship dies, your self-identity, or the way you see yourself, naturally changes.

You may have gone from being a "wife" or "husband" to a "widow" or "widower." You may have gone from being a "parent" to a "bereaved parent." The way you define yourself and the way society defines you is changed. As one woman said, "I used to have a husband and was part of a couple. Now I'm not only single, but a single parent and a widow. . . I hate that word. It makes me sound like a lonely spider."

What's more, a death often requires you to take on new roles that had been filled by the person who died. After all, someone still has to take out the garbage, someone still has to buy the groceries, someone still has to make the wi-fi work. You confront your changed identity every time you do something that used to be done by the person who died. This can be very hard work and, at times, can leave you feeling very drained of emotional, physical, and spiritual energy.

> *"Let yourself be drawn by the strange pull of what you love. It will not lead you astray."*
>
> Rumi

You may occasionally feel childlike as you struggle with your changing identity. You may feel a temporarily heightened dependence on others as well as helplessness, frustration, inadequacy, and fear. These feelings can be overwhelming and scary, but they are actually a natural response to this important need of mourning.

As you address this need, be certain to keep other major life changes to a minimum if at all possible. Now is probably not the time for a major move or career change, for example. Your energy is already likely diminished. Don't deplete it even more by making significant changes or taking on too many tasks.

Remember—do what you need to do to survive for now as you try to re-anchor yourself. To be dependent on others as you struggle with a changing identity does not make you bad or inferior. Your self-identity has been assaulted. Be compassionate with yourself. Reach out for and accept the support of others.

Many people discover that as they work on this need, they ultimately discover some positive aspects of their changed self-identity. You may develop a renewed confidence in yourself, for example. You might reveal a more caring, kind, and sensitive part of yourself. You may develop an assertive part of your identity that empowers you to go on living even though you continue to feel a sense of loss. (To learn more about the transformations that often come with grief, see Touchstone Ten.)

EXPRESS YOURSELF:
Go to *The Understanding Your Grief Journal* on pp. 116-118.

MOURNING NEED 5:

Search for Meaning

When someone you love dies, it's normal to question the meaning and purpose of life. You will probably reconsider your life philosophy and explore religious and spiritual values as you work on this need. You may discover yourself searching for meaning in your continued living as you ask "How?" and "Why" questions. "How could God let this happen?" "Why did this happen now, in this way?" The death reminds you of your lack of control. It can leave you feeling powerless.

> *"He who has a why to live can bear almost any how."*
>
> Friedrich Nietzsche

The person who died was a part of you. This death means you mourn a loss not only outside of yourself but inside of yourself as well. At times, overwhelming sadness and loneliness may be your constant companions. You may feel that when this person died, part of you died, too. And now you are faced with finding some meaning in going on with your life even though you may often feel empty.

This death calls for you to consider your spirituality. You may doubt your faith and have spiritual conflicts and questions racing through your head and heart. This is normal and part of your journey toward renewed living.

You might feel distant from your God or higher power, even questioning the very existence of God. You may rage at your God. Such feelings of doubt are normal. Remember—mourners often find themselves questioning their faith for some time before they rediscover meaning in life. But be assured: It can be done, even when you don't have all the answers.

As always, be sure to express your search for meaning outside of yourself. When thoughts and feelings about meaning and purpose naturally arise (and they will!), talk to a good listener about them. Perhaps you have one or two friends whom you think of as spiritually grounded or interested in philosophical discussions. Engage them in conversation over lunch or a cup of coffee. Or if you're struggling with practical meaning-of-life issues, such as searching for reasons to get out of bed in the morning, consider seeing a grief counselor or other care provider until you regain your footing.

Early in your grief, allow yourself to openly mourn without pressuring yourself to have answers to such profound meaning-of-life questions. Move at your own pace as you recognize that allowing yourself to hurt and finding meaning are not mutually exclusive.

TURNING TO RITUAL TO FACILITATE MOURNING

As you work on the six needs of mourning over time, actively embracing and expressing your grief, you can also add in the power of ritual to encourage your active mourning. Long after the funeral, grief rituals that combine intentionality, actions, symbolism, sequence, presence, heart, and spirit can also give your grief divine momentum.

Group memory ceremonies (sometimes orchestrated at holiday time by hospices or funeral homes); family cemetery visits, tree plantings, or memorial runs in honor of a loved one; annual fundraisers to support a nonprofit or cause dear to the person who died; and gatherings that mark the anniversary of the death are a few common examples of group rituals. Such ceremonies help grievers meet their ongoing needs of mourning. You can pick and choose the forms of ceremony that feel right for you. But you can also carry out personal grief rituals by yourself at any time in the privacy of your own home. For more guidance and ritual ideas, you might want to look over my book *Grief Day by Day: Simple Practices to Help Yourself Survive...and Thrive.*

I hope you'll try some ongoing rituals. If you do, I believe you'll marvel at their power. **Death transforms love into grief, and ritual helps transform grief into healing.**

EXPRESS YOURSELF:
Go to *The Understanding Your Grief Journal* on p. 119.

More often your need to mourn and find meaning in your continued living will blend into each other, with the former giving way to the latter as your grief work continues.

EXPRESS YOURSELF:
Go to *The Understanding Your Grief Journal* on pp. 120-122.

MOURNING NEED 6:
Let Others Help You—Now and Always

The quality and quantity of understanding support you get during your work of mourning will have a major influence on your capacity to integrate this loss into your life. You cannot—nor should you try to—do this alone. Drawing on the experiences and encouragement of friends, fellow grievers, and counselors is not a weakness but a healthy human need. And because mourning naturally unfolds over time, this support must be available long after the death of someone in your life.

Unfortunately, because our society places so much value on the ability to "carry on," "keep your chin up," and "keep busy," many grieving people are abandoned shortly after the event of the death. "It's best not to talk about it," "It's over and done with," and "It's time to get on with your life" are the types of messages directed at grieving people that all too often dominate. Obviously, this thinking encourages you to deny or repress your grief rather than embrace and express it.

If you know people who consider themselves supportive yet offer you these kinds of mourning-avoidant attitudes, you'll need to look to others for truly helpful support. People who see your mourning as something that should be overcome or gone around instead of experienced will not help you come out of the dark and into the light.

To be truly helpful, the people in your support system must appreciate the impact this death has had on you. They must understand that in order to heal, you must be allowed—even encouraged—to mourn long after the death. And they must encourage you to see mourning not as an enemy to be vanquished but rather as a necessity to be experienced as a result of having loved. Perhaps you are surrounded by just such people. If you are receiving excellent support from friends and family, you're fortunate. Have gratitude and grace.

> "Grief knits two hearts in closer bonds than happiness ever can, and common sufferings are far stronger links than common joys."
>
> Alphonse de Lamartine

You will also probably discover, if you haven't already, that you can benefit from a connectedness that comes from people who have also had a death in their lives. The credo of The Compassionate Friends, an international organization of grieving parents, is "You need not walk alone." I might add, "You cannot walk alone." Support groups, where people come together and share the common bond of experience, can be invaluable in helping you and your grief and supporting your need to mourn long after the death.

You will learn more about support groups and how to create support systems for yourself later in this book. Right now, remind yourself that you deserve and need to have understanding people around you who allow you to feel and share your grief long after our culture tends to deem appropriate.

EXPRESS YOURSELF:
Go to *The Understanding Your Grief Journal* on pp. 123-124.

Journeying with the Six Needs

I've been a grief educator for four decades, and I've found that mourners are often helped by the concept of the six central needs of mourning. There is a lot of information in this book, but if you were to commit to memory one small part, I would recommend that it be the six needs of mourning. Upholding and fulfilling these six needs over time will help you understand how you have been transformed by this loss. I would also encourage you to revisit this chapter now and then in the future and review your progress in meeting these needs.

The consequences of *not* attending to the six needs of mourning, on the other hand, can be devastating. If you don't actively engage with and express the six needs of mourning on an ongoing basis, as needed, you may remain stuck or lost in the wilderness of your grief. I'll talk more about this in Touchstone Eight, but for now, I hope you'll remember that the six needs are your guide and your friend.

Recognize You Are Not Crazy

In all my years as a grief counselor, the most common question grieving people have asked me is, "Am I going crazy?" The second most common is, "Am I normal?" The journey through grief can be so radically different from our everyday realities that sometimes it feels more like being picked up and dropped onto the surface of the moon than it does a trek through the wilderness. The terrain can be so very foreign and disorienting, and our behaviors in that terrain can feel so out of the ordinary, that we often feel like we're going crazy.

> "Grief can derange even the strongest and most disciplined of minds."
>
> George R.R. Martin

I once had the honor of companioning a man whose wife had died. Before her death, they frequently ran errands and drove places together in their car, he at the wheel and she in the passenger seat. Each time they parked outside their destination, the man would turn to his wife and ask, "Do you think we should lock the car?" and his wife would answer, "What's the point? We don't have anything worth stealing." Then, without further ado, they would get out of the car, lock it, and go about their business. This ritual had started early in their fifty-year marriage and had continued until she died.

After her death, the husband continued to drive and do the errands. Whenever he stopped and parked, his body would instinctively pivot to the right, and he would start to say aloud, "Do you think we should..." Then he would sit in his car and cry. He would also wonder if he was going crazy.

The widower told his friends about his ongoing compulsion to carry out the car-locking routine. He was expressing a part of his grief outside of himself, and he was reaching out for help. But as too often happens in our mourning-avoidant culture, instead of affirming that continuing to search and yearn was natural and that they were there to bear witness to his normal and necessary grief, his friends told him he was going crazy and should see a grief counselor.

And so it was that he came to see me. What a privilege to help this man talk out his grief. I was able to normalize his car-locking ritual by helping him understand that it was allowing him to integrate the reality of the death. He wasn't going crazy! His instinct to continue to turn to his wife was very normal, and in grief, learning to follow your instincts is more than half the battle.

This man wasn't crazy, and you're not either. You may be experiencing thoughts and feelings that *seem* crazy because they are so unusual to you, but what is unusual in life is often usual in grief.

This touchstone helps you be on the lookout for the trail marker that affirms your sanity: Recognize You Are Not Crazy. It's an important trail marker, because if you miss it, your entire journey through the wilderness of your grief may feel like Alice's surreal visit to Wonderland. Actually, your journey may still *feel* surreal even if you find this trail marker, but at least you'll understand cognitively that you're not going crazy.

Following are a number of common thoughts and feelings in grief that cause mourners to feel like they're going crazy. They may or may not be a part of your personal experience. As I've said, my intent is not to prescribe what should be happening to you. Instead, I encourage you to become familiar with what you *may* encounter while you grieve and do your work of mourning.

> *"Whole years of joy glide unperceived away, while sorrow counts the minutes as they pass."*
>
> William Howard

Time Distortion

"I don't know what day it is, let alone what time it is!" This kind of comment is not unusual in grief. Sometimes time moves quickly; at other times, it crawls. Your sense of past and future also may seem muddled or frozen in place. You may lose track of what day or even what month it is. Your potential inability to keep track of time right now isn't crazy. It's common in grief, particularly in the early days and weeks after a death.

EXPRESS YOURSELF:
Go to your *Understanding Your Grief Journal* on p. 126.

Self-Focus

Especially early in your grief, you may find yourself being less aware of the needs of others than you usually are. You may not want to listen to other people's problems. You might not have the energy to attend to all the needs of your children, other family members, friends, or colleagues. You may feel flabbergasted that the world around you is still turning while your life is at a complete standstill.

The compulsion to focus only on your own thoughts and feelings doesn't mean you're going crazy. What it does mean is that you need to focus on yourself right now. Your mind and spirit are directing your attention away from others and toward yourself because you need this self-focus to integrate your grief. As we discussed in Misconception 11 in Touchstone Two, don't feel guilty or selfish about these feelings. They are necessary for your survival. Your willingness to prioritize caring for yourself now is what will allow you to reconnect with others later on and return to supporting them in their daily lives and life trials.

Of course, if you are a primary caregiver for children, elderly parents, or others, and your need to self-focus right now is making it impossible for you to provide them with good care for the time being, it's also essential that you solicit extra help. Don't feel bad if you're a grieving caregiver who needs to step away from some of your caregiving responsibilities for a time. You need and deserve respite and intensive care yourself at the moment, so it's perfectly understandable to ask others to help out however they can.

Still, some people may try to take your grief away from you by discouraging or shaming you for any kind of self-focus. They may want you to quickly reenter the regular world because they don't understand your need for temporary retreat.

The word "temporary" is important here. You may move back and forth between needing time alone and needing time with other people. If you stay only in a self-focused, inward mode, you risk developing a pattern of not sharing your grief. As you know by now, not sharing your grief is a mistake that will inhibit your ability to integrate this loss into your life.

When you are in pain following the death of someone loved, the turning inward and the need for self-focus are analogous to what occurs when you have a serious physical wound. You cover a cut or gash with a bandage for a period of time, right? Then only later do you expose the scabbed-over wound to the open air, which further helps with healing. The wound of grief certainly demands this same sequence of care.

EXPRESS YOURSELF:
Go to your *Understanding Your Grief Journal* on p. 126.

Rethinking and Retelling Your Story

In Touchstone Three we talked about the importance of thinking about and telling your story. Here I want to remind you that if you're feeling compelled to do these things quite a lot, it doesn't mean you're going crazy. In fact, it means you're doing the necessary work of mourning.

Whether you're conscious of this fact or not, you tell yourself and others the story in an effort to integrate it into your life. What has happened to you—the death of someone you love—is so hard to fathom that your mind compels you to revisit it and revisit it and revisit it until you've truly acknowledged and embraced it. And over time, remembering and telling the story helps bring your head and your heart together.

Allow yourself this necessary repetition. Blocking it out won't help you heal. Don't be angry with yourself if you can't seem to stop wanting to repeat your story, whether in your own mind or aloud to others.

Yes, it hurts to constantly think and talk about the person you love so much. But remember—grief wounds often get worse before they get better. Be compassionate with yourself. Try to surround yourself with people who allow and encourage you to repeat whatever you need to repeat. Support groups are helpful to many grievers because members share a mutual understanding of the need to tell the story and to have others listen. Grace happens!

> *"Give sorrow words; the grief that does not speak knits up the o'er-wrought heart and bids it break."*
>
> William Shakespeare

Still, I know that sometimes grievers get stuck on thoughts about a certain aspect of the death or relationship. If you feel like you're caught up in a loop of thinking or talking about a particular facet of the story or events, especially if it's distressing to you, I encourage you to reach out to a grief counselor. You may simply need a little extra help integrating that particular chapter so that the momentum of healthy mourning can continue to carry you forward in your journey.

EXPRESS YOURSELF:
Go to *The Understanding Your Grief Journal* on p. 127.

Sudden Changes in Mood

When someone loved dies, you may feel like you're surviving fairly well one minute and in the depths of despair the next. Sudden mood changes can be a difficult yet normal part of your grief journey. They might be small or dramatic. They can be triggered by anything— driving past a familiar place, a song, an insensitive comment, or even a change in the weather.

Mood changes can make you feel like you're going crazy because your inappropriate self-expectation may be that you should follow a pattern of continuous motion forward in grief. In other words, you may expect yourself to keep feeling better and better. In reality, grief twists and turns like a mountainous trail. One minute you might be feeling great and the next lousy. Again, in general, grief usually gets worse before it gets better.

So if you have these ups and downs, don't be hard on yourself. Instead, practice patience. As you do the work of mourning and move toward healing, any periods of hopelessness will more and more be replaced by periods of hopefulness.

EXPRESS YOURSELF:
Go to *The Understanding Your Grief Journal* on p. 128.

Powerlessness and Helplessness

Your grief can at times leave you feeling powerless. You may think or say, "What am I going to do? I feel so completely helpless." The experience of helplessness sometimes makes us think we're going crazy because we often get used to long stretches in our lives when most everything seems steady or more or less the same. Then when the death of someone loved tips the boat, we may naturally find ourselves floundering and sputtering.

> *"Grief is a most peculiar thing; we're so helpless in the face of it. It's like a window that will simply open of its own accord. The room grows cold, and we can do nothing but shiver."*
>
> John Irving

While part of you realizes you had no control over what happened, another part feels a sense of powerlessness at not having been able to prevent it. You would like to have your life back the way it was, but you can't. You may think, hope, wish, and pray the death could be reversed while all the time feeling powerless in the knowledge that it can't.

Also, you may wonder that if somehow you had acted differently or been more assertive, you could have prevented the death. Your "if-onlys" and "what-ifs" are often expressions of wishing you could have been more powerful or in control of something you could not. Lack of control is a difficult reality to accept, yet it is one that over time and through the work of mourning you must encounter. These feelings of helplessness and powerlessness in the face of this painful reality are normal and natural.

Almost paradoxically, by acknowledging and allowing for temporary feelings of helplessness, you help yourself. When you try to "stay strong," you often get yourself into trouble. Instead, surrender to your vulnerability. Share your feelings with caring people around you. Remember—shared grief is diminished grief; find someone to talk to who will listen without judging.

EXPRESS YOURSELF:
Go to *The Understanding Your Grief Journal* on p. 128.

Grief Attacks or Griefbursts

"I was doing pretty well, when out of nowhere came this overwhelming wave of grief!" Has this happened to you?

> *"Grief is like the ocean; it comes on waves, ebbing and flowing. Sometimes the water is calm, and sometimes it is overwhelming. All we can do is learn to swim."*
>
> Vicki Harrison

I call this experience a "griefburst"—a sudden, sharp feeling of grief that causes anxiety and pain. Some people call them grief attacks because they often attack without warning.

Before they come to grief, many people expect grief to be made up mostly of long periods of deep depression. Actually, after the early weeks, what you're more likely to encounter are acute and episodic pangs or spasms of grief in between relatively pain-free hours.

During a griefburst, you may feel an overwhelming sense of missing the person you love and find yourself openly crying or sobbing. As one widow told me, "I'll be busy for a while, and sometimes even forget he has died. Then I'll see his picture or smell his favorite food, and I'll just feel like I can't even move."

Griefbursts may feel like "crazybursts," but they're normal. When and if one strikes you, be compassionate with yourself. You have every right to experience intense pangs of missing the person who died and to feel temporary paralysis or loss of control. Whatever you do, don't try to deny or suppress a griefburst when it comes on. It's powerful because it wants and needs your attention. I also like to think of griefbursts as evidence that those we love are determined not to be forgotten.

Although the pain of a griefburst hurts so deeply, allow it to wash over you. If you'd feel more comfortable, retreat to a private place where you can wail or scream or do whatever you need to do. After it passes, talk about your griefburst with someone who cares about you.

EXPRESS YOURSELF:
Go to *The Understanding Your Grief Journal* on p. 128.

Crying and Sobbing

We already discussed the importance of tears of grief in Touchstone Two (see p. 36). But here I'd like to briefly revisit this topic as it pertains to feelings of going crazy.

If you're crying and sobbing a lot, you may feel like you're out of control, which can in turn trigger feeling crazy. But sobbing and wailing come from the inner core of your being. They are expressions of true, deep, strong emotions within you. These emotions need to get out, and sobbing allows for their release.

> "But there was no need to be ashamed of tears, for tears bore witness that a man had the greatest of courage: the courage to suffer."
>
> Viktor Frankl

In many Eastern cultures, sobbing and wailing (sometimes called "keening") are encouraged and understood as a normal part of grief and mourning. In our culture, however, sobbing is often seen as frightening. It is perceived as being out of control. (That's where your griefburst-related feelings of loss of control come from!) But it is actually this very loss of control that helps you express strong feelings. Your feelings are too strong to be under control inside you—and their authentic expression can't be under control outside of you, either.

If you're crying or sobbing a lot, you're not crazy. Cry, wail, and sob as long and as hard and as often as you need to. Don't try to be strong and brave for yourself or others. Tears have a voice of their own. You will be wise to allow yours to speak to you.

EXPRESS YOURSELF:
Go to *The Understanding Your Grief Journal* on p. 129.

BORROWED TEARS

Here's another kind of crying that can make you feel like you're going crazy: borrowed tears. Borrowed tears are those that spring up when you're suddenly and often unexpectedly touched by something you might see, hear, or smell, and you react with strong emotion. During a griefburst, you might be brought to tears by a place or a smell that reminds you of the person who died. Borrowed tears, on the other hand, seem to come out of nowhere and are triggered by something you don't associate with the person who died and wouldn't normally be upset by.

Borrowed tears are called this because you seem to be borrowing them from someone else's store of pain and memory. They're not yours! For example, you might find yourself crying at a sappy TV commercial or seeing a little bird out your window. These things never made you sad before. Why are you crying now?

You're crying because your heart and soul are hurting and your emotions are tender. Think of it this way: If you press on your leg gently with your hand, it doesn't hurt. But if you break your leg and then press on it, even the slightest touch can hurt. Your heart is broken now, and anything that touches your heart even slightly (including happy or beautiful things) may hurt a lot. This is normal and will soften as you allow yourself to mourn.

Linking Objects

Linking objects are items that belonged to the person who died that you now like to have around you. Objects such as clothing, books, knick-knacks, furniture, artwork, and other prized possessions can help you feel physically closer to the person you miss so much.

Once when I was counseling a widow, she shared with me that she found it comforting to take one of her husband's shirts to bed with her. She said that as she clutched his shirt close to her, she didn't feel so alone. And as she worked through her grief over time, her need for the shirt faded.

If you like to hold, be near, look at, sleep with, caress, or smell a special belonging of the person who died, you're not crazy. You're simply trying to hold on to a tangible, physical connection to the person. The person's body is no longer physically here, but these special items are. Like the woman who slept with her husband's shirt, you'll probably need your linking objects less and less over time, as you integrate the loss into your life. But you may always find these items special, and you may always want to keep them.

I would also advise not to rush into giving away the belongings of the person who died. Sometimes people hurry into clearing out all the "stuff" because they think it will help them "move on." It doesn't. In fact, getting rid of the belongings because they're too painful to have around is antithetical to the touchstones described in this book. For example, opening to the presence of the loss often includes embracing the feelings that are stirred up by the belongings of the person who died. If you get rid of the belongings prematurely, you in effect rid yourself of a natural and necessary medium of healing.

I'd also like to point out the difference between cherishing some belongings and creating a shrine. Mourners create a shrine when for years (sometimes decades) after a death they keep everything in a room or a part of their home just as it was when the person died. Unlike cherishing particular linking objects, creating a shrine often prevents you from acknowledging the painful new reality that someone you love has died. It's as if you still expect the person to return at any moment.

> "Death ends
> a life, not a
> relationship."
>
> Morrie Schwartz

I do think it's OK for mourners to leave the belongings of the person who died just as they were for a period of time after the death. In the early weeks and months of grief, you may simply lack the energy to contend with the person's belongings, and your feelings of shock and denial may, in some circumstances, be so powerful that you simply can't bring yourself to confront the person's clothing, furniture, keepsakes, etc. for a while. Within reason, go at your own pace, and err on the side of caution. I often say that there are no rewards for speed, and once you've disposed of something, you can't get it back.

EXPRESS YOURSELF:
Go to *The Understanding Your Grief Journal* on p. 129.

> "Your body is
> so very wise. It
> will try to slow
> you down and
> invite you to
> authentically
> mourn the losses
> that touch your
> life. The emotions
> of grief are
> often expressed
> as bodily-felt
> energies."
>
> Alan D. Wolfelt

Identification Symptoms of Physical Illness

When you care deeply about someone and they die, you sometimes develop new ways to identify with and feel close to that person. One subconscious way is by relating to the physical symptoms of the person who died. For example, if she died from a brain tumor, you may find yourself having headaches. If he had a heart attack, you may experience chest pains. Of course, checking for genuine physical problems is important; do go get a thorough check-up if you're having any troubling symptoms. But you also should be aware that you might be experiencing identification symptoms of physical illness.

Grieving people have shared with me these examples:

"She had awful pains in her stomach, and after she died I began to have them, too. It kind of made me feel close to her, actually. After a while the pains went away, and I felt some sense of loss that they did. As I've healed, I've been able to let go of the stomach pain."

"I loved him so much. After he died, I wanted to be close to him. I guess one of the ways I did it was to be dizzy just like he used to be all the time."

Don't be shocked if you have any physical symptoms that are similar to those experienced by the person who died. You're not crazy. Your body is simply responding to the loss. As you do the hard work of mourning, however, these symptoms should go away. If they don't, in addition to seeing your primary-care provider to rule out any physical problems, find someone who will listen to you and help you understand what is happening.

EXPRESS YOURSELF:
Go to *The Understanding Your Grief Journal* on p. 130.

Suicidal Thoughts

We touched on suicidal thoughts in Touchstone Four, but this subject is important enough to reemphasize here. Thoughts that come and go about questioning if you want to go on living can be a normal part of grief and mourning. You might say or think something on the order of, "It'd be so much easier to not be here." Usually this thought is not so much an active wish to die as it is a wish to ease your pain.

Having these passing thoughts is normal and not crazy. However, making plans or taking action to end your life is abnormal. Sometimes your body, mind, and spirit can hurt so much that you wonder if you will ever feel alive again. You may also feel like you can't imagine regaining the drive to keep living and to find meaning again. Just remember that if you do the hard work of befriending and mourning your grief, you can and will find continued meaning in life. In the meantime, reach out for help and borrow hope whenever you need to.

If thoughts of suicide take on planning and structure, make certain that you get help immediately. Sometimes tunnel vision can temporarily prevent you from seeing choices or the bigger picture. Please choose to go on living as you honor the life and memory of the person who died.

EXPRESS YOURSELF:
Go to *The Understanding Your Grief Journal* on p. 130.

Drug or Alcohol Use

When someone loved dies, you may be tempted to quickly quell your feelings of grief. This desire to avoid and mask the pain is understandable. The trouble is, using drugs and alcohol to help you do so only brings temporary relief from a hurt that must ultimately be embraced.

A well-meaning friend hands you a bottle of sleeping pills and says, "Take one tonight. You need your sleep." Your doctor quickly prescribes an antidepressant, promising it will make you feel better. Or you find yourself sipping wine to get through each evening. Should you take these substances?

First, never take prescription drugs unless they were prescribed for you by a medical provider. You don't know how you might react to a certain medication.

Don't take a drug that your doctor has prescribed, either, unless you understand and agree with the reasons for taking it and the effects it may have on you. If you need more information, ask. Drugs that make you feel numb or unnaturally peaceful may only complicate your grief experience. After all, they will eventually wear off, and you will still have to struggle with the pain. Psychological or physical dependence can also be a problem with many medications. If your doctor has prescribed a drug to help you cope with your grief, you may want to get a second opinion.

Alcohol is yet another danger for grieving people. When you drink, you may indeed feel better—temporarily. But alcohol taken to mask painful feelings is only a crutch and when overused, may in fact cause an entirely new set of problems. The same goes for marijuana and other controlled substances.

This is not to say that grieving people should never take medications, however. You may, for example, become so sleep-deprived that *temporary* use of a sedative, anti-anxiety medication, or sleep aid is warranted. And of course, if clinical depression arises, taking prescribed antidepressants may well be an essential, lifesaving part of your care plan. It is also important to note that people who were taking antidepressants prior to the death of someone loved should continue taking them afterward as ordered by a physician. Your grief will *not* be further complicated by the use of these medications.

In general, though, taking alcohol and drugs is an ineffective, counterproductive, and potentially harmful way to cope with grief. Instead of relying on their deceptive comfort, I urge you to turn to your fellow human beings for support. Reconciliation of grief comes through the ongoing expression of thoughts and feelings, not through their drug-induced repression.

EXPRESS YOURSELF:
Go to *The Understanding Your Grief Journal* on p. 131.

Dreams

Dreaming a lot about the person who died can contribute to your feelings of going crazy. Mourners sometimes tell me that they can't stop thinking about the death—even in their sleep!

Keep in mind, though, that dreams are one of the ways the work of mourning takes place. A dream may reflect a searching for the person who died, for example. You may dream that you are with them in a crowded place then lose them and cannot find them. Dreams also provide opportunities—to feel close to the person who died, to embrace the reality of the death, to gently confront the depth of the loss, to renew memories, or to develop a new self-identity. Dreams also may help you search for meaning in life and death or explore unfinished business. Finally, dreams can even show you hope for the future.

> *"In the garden of memory, in the palace of dreams, that is where you and I shall meet."*
>
> Lewis Carroll

The content of your dreams often reflects changes in your grief journey. You may have one kind of dream early in your grief and another later on. So if dreams are part of your trek through the wilderness, make use of them to better understand where you have been, where you are, and where you are going. Also, find a skilled listener who won't interpret your dreams for you but who will listen to you talk about them.

Of course, nightmares are also a possibility in grief, particularly after a traumatic or violent death. These types of dreams can be very frightening and disturbing. If your dreams are distressing, talk about them with someone who can support and understand you, and if they continue, reach out to a grief counselor. **In general, if any facet of your grief starts to feel overwhelming or especially troubling to you, that's a sign that it's probably a good time to see a counselor for a few sessions, just as you would see a doctor if you were having overwhelming or especially troubling physical symptoms.**

EXPRESS YOURSELF:
Go to *The Understanding Your Grief Journal* on p. 131.

Mystical Experiences

When someone you love dies, you may have experiences that are not always rationally explainable. That doesn't mean you're crazy!

If you share these experiences with others, they may question your mental fitness, however. But I like to say that if you have mystical experiences, you're simply mystically sensitive.

The primary form of mystical experience that grieving people have taught me about is communicating with the person who died. This ranges from sensing a presence or feeling a touch to hearing a voice, seeing a vision, receiving a sign, and many more.

What constitutes a mystical experience in grief can vary greatly. In Alabama, for example, a mother whose daughter had died woke up one summer morning only to find it snowing in her backyard (and her backyard only)! The snow lasted for fifteen minutes and then stopped. The mother understood this as a communication telling her that her daughter was all right and that she shouldn't worry so much. In another instance, a man whose wife had died saw her lying on the couch in their living room. "It's like she came to me and wrapped me in her arms. I felt warm and happy…I experienced her presence," he said.

Some people find these experiences hard to believe and explain them away in a rational manner: "I must have been dreaming" or "I was probably half-asleep." Others try to distance themselves from these experiences because they have been taught that such things are impossible: "A rational mind just doesn't experience those kinds of things." So, if you want to be considered rational or sane (and who doesn't!), you might feel compelled to distance yourself from these kinds of experiences.

But I have listened to and learned from hundreds of people who believe they have received some form of communication from those who have died. If you count yourself among them, you're not going crazy. You can still be very sane and exceedingly rational while at times experiencing and embracing mystical encounters. Who on this earth is to say what's real and what isn't? Certainly not I. Remain open to these experiences, and be thankful for any comfort they provide.

EXPRESS YOURSELF:
Go to *The Understanding Your Grief Journal* on p. 132.

Anniversaries, Holidays, and Special Occasions

Naturally, holidays and special occasions can bring about pangs of grief or full-on griefbursts. Birthdays, wedding dates, holidays such as Thanksgiving, Hanukkah, and Christmas, and other special occasions typically give rise to a heightened sense of loss.

Your grief may also grow more pronounced in any circumstances that bring up reminders of the painful absence of someone in your life. For many families, certain days have special meaning (for example, the beginning of spring, the first snowfall, an annual Fourth of July party, or any time when activities were shared as a couple or a family), and the person who died is more deeply missed at those times.

> *"One missing bulb keeps the rest from lighting."*
>
> Author unknown

If you find yourself having a really tough time on special days, you're not crazy. Perhaps the most important thing to remember is that your feelings are natural. And sometimes the anticipation of an anniversary or holiday turns out to be worse than the day itself.

Interestingly, sometimes your internal clock may alert you to an anniversary date you may not have been consciously aware of beforehand. If you notice you're feeling down or experiencing deep grief, you may be having an anniversary response. Take a look at the calendar and think about if this particular day has meant anything to you in years past.

I recommend planning ahead when you know some naturally painful times are coming. In advance, think about ways you could integrate healthy mourning as well as grief support into those days. Alert the people who care about you that you'll need their understanding and empathy. Unfortunately, some grieving people will choose not to mention special dates to friends and family members, so they end up suffering in silence, and their feelings of isolation and craziness increase. My hope is that this does not happen to you and that you will get the support you need and deserve during these special times.

EXPRESS YOURSELF:
Go to *The Understanding Your Grief Journal* on p. 133.

The Crazy Things People Say and Do

Sometimes in grief, other people may make you feel crazy—like the friends of the car-locking man at the beginning of this chapter. When what you really need is acceptance, affirmation, and nonjudgment, they may instead imply or outright tell you that your natural grief response is abnormal or wrong in some way.

Platitudes are one way this can happen. You've probably heard some of these gems:

"At least you had him as long as you did."

"I guess God needed her in heaven."

"He's in a better place."

"Just keep your chin up!"

"Well, he lived to be 89."

"Time heals all wounds."

"He wouldn't want you to be sad."

"It could be worse."

These and other clichés are harmful to grievers because they essentially minimize or try to shut down your normal grief. And when this happens, it might make you feel a little crazy because everyone's telling you one thing while your internal reality is completely the opposite.

In addition to saying unempathetic things, some people around you may at times do hurtful things as well. They might avoid you or pretend nothing's wrong. They might become inappropriately, selfishly emotional in your presence, forcing you to comfort them instead of the other way around. They might give you an insensitive gift. They might blame you or put more of a burden on you in some way through their actions. And when such things happen, you might feel like it's your instinctual reaction to what they've done that's off-kilter.

Just remember that when it comes to grief, it's our culture that's crazy, not you. And that's why people so often say and do hurtful things to grievers—because the culture is generally not teaching them loss-related emotional intelligence. Most of these people are well-intentioned, however, so we sometimes have to take a deep breath and remind ourselves to have grace. They know not what they do.

EXPRESS YOURSELF:
Go to *The Understanding Your Grief Journal* on pp. 133-134.

You're Not Crazy, You're Grieving

Never forget that your journey through the wilderness of your grief may bring you through all kinds of strange and unfamiliar terrain. As I said at the beginning of this touchstone, your experiences may feel so alien that you feel more like you're on the moon!

When you feel like you're going crazy, remind yourself to look for the trail marker that assures you you're *not* going crazy. You're grieving. The two can feel remarkably similar sometimes.

Nurture Yourself

Again, the word "bereaved," which to our modern-day ears can sound like an old-fashioned term, means "to be torn apart" and "to have special needs." Perhaps your most important special need right now is to be compassionate with yourself. In fact, the word "compassion" means "with empathy." Caring for and about yourself with great empathy is self-compassion.

> *"Self-care is giving the world the best of you instead of what's left of you."*
>
> Katie Reed

This touchstone is a gentle reminder to be kind to yourself as you journey through the wilderness of your grief. If you were embarking on a hike of many days through the rugged, high-altitude mountains of Colorado, would you dress scantily, carry little water, and push yourself until you dropped? Of course not. You would prepare carefully and proceed cautiously. You would take care of yourself because if you didn't, you could die. The consequences of not taking care of yourself in grief can be equally devastating.

Yet over many years of walking with people in grief, I have discovered that most of us are hard on ourselves when we're in mourning. We judge ourselves and we shame ourselves and we take care of ourselves last. But good self-care is essential to your survival. To practice good self-care doesn't mean you're feeling sorry for yourself or being self-indulgent; rather, it means you're creating conditions that allow you to integrate the death of someone loved into your heart and soul.

I believe that it is only in nurturing ourselves, in allowing ourselves the time and loving attention we need to journey safely and deeply through grief, that we can find meaning in our continued living. We have all heard the words, "Blessed are those who mourn, for they shall be comforted." To this I might add, "Blessed are those who learn self-compassion during times of grief, for they shall go on to discover continued meaning in life, living, and loving."

Remember—self-care fortifies your long and challenging grief journey, a journey that leaves you profoundly affected and deeply changed. To be self-nurturing is to have the courage to pay attention to and honor your needs. Above all, self-nurturing is about self-acceptance. When we recognize that grief care begins with ourselves, we no longer think of those around us as being responsible for our wellbeing. Healthy self-care forces us to mourn in ways that help us heal, and that is nurturing indeed.

I also believe that self-nurturing is about celebration, about taking time to enjoy the moment, to find hidden treasures everywhere—a child's smile, a beautiful sunrise, a flower in bloom, a friend's gentle touch. Grief teaches us the importance of living fully in the present while also remembering our past and embracing our future.

Walt Whitman wrote, "I celebrate myself." In caring for yourself with empathy, you are celebrating life as a human being who has suffered grief and come to recognize that the preciousness of life is a superb opportunity for celebration.

EXPRESS YOURSELF:
Go to *The Understanding Your Grief Journal* on pp. 136-137.

FIRST AID FOR BROKEN HEARTS

When your heart is broken, you need first aid. You need immediate, practical, hands-on care.

If you fell from a ladder and broke your arm, you would head to urgent care. Yet many people with broken hearts try to ignore their injuries and continue on with their lives as best they can. They don't get immediate care. They don't seek first aid. And it's a mistake that costs them the fullness of life.

But here you are, reading this book and seeking first aid. You are not making the mistake of neglecting your wounds. You are being wise in giving attention to the reality of how you have been "torn apart."

You'll find more encouraging thoughts on this topic in my resource, *First Aid for Broken Hearts*—a small, illustrated book to keep on your coffee table or gift to someone in need.

Nurturing Your Whole Self

We tend to think of grief as an emotional experience. It is indeed that, but it's more than that. The profound grief that follows the death of someone loved deeply affects us physically, cognitively, socially, and spiritually, as well. In other words, grief is a holistic experience, which means when we are grieving, our self-care must also be holistic.

What follows is a brief introduction to caring for each of these facets of your self. You will then be invited to go to your companion journal and express how you see yourself doing in each of these areas.

NURTURING YOURSELF PHYSICALLY

As you're journeying through grief, your body may be letting you know it feels distressed, too. Actually, one literal definition of the word "grievous" is "causing physical suffering." You may be shocked by how much your body responds to the impact of your loss.

Among the most common physical responses to loss are troubles with sleeping and low energy. You may have difficulty getting to sleep. Perhaps even more commonly, you may be waking up early in the morning and having trouble getting back to sleep. The problem is, when you're grieving your body needs more rest than usual, not less. In general, you may find yourself tiring more quickly—sometimes even at the start of the day. **This is called the lethargy of grief, and it's a natural mechanism intended to slow you down and encourage you to care for your body.**

> "And no one ever told me about the laziness of grief."
>
> C.S. Lewis

But even if you're fatigued, you may not be sleeping well. Many people in grief experience sleep disturbance. If you think about it, sleeping is a primary way in which we routinely release control. But when someone in your life dies, you feel a loss of control. You may not want to lose any more control by sleeping. The need to stay awake may also relate to the fear of additional losses. If you stay awake and vigilant, you may feel you can help prevent more loss. Some grieving people have even taught me that they stay awake hoping to not miss the person who died in case they return or offer a sign. All of these sleep-depriving rationales—whether they're conscious or subconscious—are normal and understandable.

You may also feel unwell. Muscle aches and pains, shortness of breath, feelings of emptiness in your stomach, tightness in your throat or chest, digestive problems, sensitivity to noise, heart palpitations, queasiness, nausea, headaches, increased allergic reactions, changes in appetite, weight loss or gain, agitation, and generalized tension—these are all ways your body may react to the death of someone loved.

What's more, if you have a chronic existing health issue, it may become worse. The stress of grief can suppress your immune system, elevate stress chemicals like cortisol, and make you more susceptible to physical problems.

Right now you may not feel in control of how your body is responding, but keep in mind that it's communicating with you about the stress you're experiencing. Most of the time, the physical symptoms we've been reviewing here are normal and temporary.

Still, good physical self-care is important at this time. Your body is the house you live in. Just as your house requires care and maintenance to protect you from the outside elements, your body requires that you honor it and treat it with respect. The quality of your life ahead depends on how you take care of your body today. This includes openly expressing your grief. Many grieving people have taught me that if they avoid or repress talking about the death, their bodies begin to express their grief for them.

TWELVE COMMANDMENTS OF GOOD HEALTH

The following imperatives are good advice for anyone, but especially for anyone in mourning. While this is by no means an all-inclusive list, it should get you off to a good start. At least, that is my hope for you.

1. Stop smoking right now

If you smoke, quitting can add years to your life. The main ways smoking kills are by heart disease, lung disease, and cancer. Tobacco use kills more than 540,000 Americans every year, making it one of the leading causes of premature death in the United States. And it leaves many others with debilitating, chronic illnesses. Vaping nicotine carries many of the same health risks. But because nicotine is so addictive, quitting cold turkey rarely works. Instead, try a smoking cessation program. Combining quit-smoking products with professional support gives you the best odds of breaking free.

> *"Climb the mountains and get their good tidings. Nature's peace will flow into you as sunshine flows into trees. The winds will blow their freshness into you, and the storms their energy, while cares will drop off like falling leaves."*
>
> John Muir

2. Eat less bad fat

Perhaps you realize you should eat less animal fat, but you eat it anyway. Why? Because it tastes good, and it's a habit. In rebuttal: There are a lot of other things that taste good, and you can change bad habits. Bad fats clog your arteries and cause heart attacks and strokes. Foods high in saturated fats are the worst offenders. These include fatty meats, butter, and full-fat cheeses.

In lieu of overindulging in bad fats, strive to eat a healthy, well-balanced diet.

3. Exercise your heart

Think of your heart as the engine in your car. Let's say you abuse it by driving it tens of thousands of miles and never performing maintenance on it. And then one day in the middle of a drive, it just stops. Don't abuse your heart. It's the engine that keeps you alive.

Each day it beats one-hundred thousand times and pumps sixteen-hundred gallons of blood over sixty-thousand miles of vessels. Your heart is your best friend. Support it every chance you have.

One way to support your heart is to move your body. Aerobic exercise—which is any activity that raises your heart rate and makes breathing harder—trains your heart, your blood vessels, and your lungs in ways that they can deliver more oxygen faster and more efficiently to your body. Just thirty minutes of exercise most days of the week can keep your heart and lungs healthy. Get clearance from your primary-care provider, then do what you most enjoy. Walking, jogging, swimming, and cycling are good forms of aerobic exercise.

4. Exercise your muscles
The American College of Sports Medicine now recommends weight training for every adult. The earlier you start, the more muscle you'll retain in older age.

There are two aspects to muscle fitness: endurance and strength. In a weight-training program, lifting lighter weights with more repetitions increases endurance, while lifting heavier weights with fewer repetitions increases strength. As you age, muscle strength declines more quickly than endurance.

Muscle conditioning is vitally important yet often neglected. The reality is that if you don't use your muscles, you'll lose your muscles. Get help from a professional trainer to assist you in creating the right weight-training program for you.

5. Exercise your mind and spirit
The demands of grief—on top of your everyday commitments—prime you for plenty of stress. Building in some regular physical exercise allows you to get away from the demands of an all-too-often hectic life, and it enhances your sense of wellbeing.

Exercise has a calming effect on the body and the mind. We know that people who regularly exercise say they handle pressure better, feel more confident, and are happier and less depressed than those who don't exercise. In other words, exercise not only benefits the body, it benefits the mind and the spirit.

6. Get adequate sleep

While you may naturally be having trouble sleeping, sleep is necessary. It gives your mind and body a chance to perform day-to-day maintenance and repairs.

When possible, try to go to bed at a similar time each night, and get up at a similar time each morning. Put away electronics and begin to completely relax an hour or so before you go to bed. Limit caffeine and alcohol intake.

If you're not sleeping well, see your primary-care provider for sleep troubleshooting and support. You won't be able to effectively work on the six needs of mourning if you're not getting enough good sleep.

And when you're feeling the natural lethargy of grief, be sure to lie down several times a day. Even if you don't fall asleep, your body needs the rest.

7. Establish a relationship with a physician

Speaking of primary-care providers—making your health a priority requires having a relationship with a trusted physician. Do you know that some people spend more time selecting a veterinarian for their pets than they do selecting a primary-care provider for their bodies? That's if they pick one at all.

Simple as it may seem, finding and making use of a good doctor can be one of the most practical, effective steps toward leading a healthier and longer life. Think of primary-care providers as coaches—trained professionals—who know how to help keep you healthy. If you don't already have one, find one now and work to create a health partnership.

8. Stay hydrated

Many people aren't aware that one of the easiest ways to stay healthy is to drink lots of water. Think of water as the oil that lubricates the mind and the body. The universal recommendation is six to eight glasses (ten-to-twelve ounces each) of water a day.

9. Slow down

Being too busy to see a doctor is only one symptom of a fast-paced, hurry-up lifestyle. For many people, the feeling of being rushed permeates their entire life. Are you living out the squeeze-it-all-in mentality? Are you simply too busy? Do you have to leave one commitment early to rush to another?

If you can allow yourself to slow down, your perception will change. Life will become easier and more enjoyable. You will work smarter. You will discover that your quality of life is generated from within instead of being imposed from the outside. As you slow down you may find that much of what you previously thought was essential can actually be postponed, delegated, or even ignored. Instead of waiting to enjoy your life someday, when everything is accomplished, allow yourself to enjoy the journey.

10. Spend time in nature

Unfortunately, most of us today are nature-deprived. We now interact with technology more than we do with anything else in our environment or with our fellow human beings. Researchers have learned that our current lack of connection with nature has caused widespread anxiety, depression, and attention disorders.

So regardless of the setting or season, put down your devices and get outside for at least twenty minutes a day. Your blood pressure and heart rate will drop, your cortisol levels will fall, you'll get the sunlight you need to regulate your sleep cycle, your cognitive stress will dissipate, your mood and self-esteem will improve, and you'll feel more in touch with your spiritual self.

11. Laugh—a lot

It turns out that humor is good medicine. Research shows that laughter stimulates chemicals in the brain that actually suppress stress-related hormones. Also, breathing and circulation are both enhanced through laughter.

If you're in deep grief, you may not feel like laughing very much right now. But as your journey progresses and whenever you can, find ways to welcome laughter into your life.

12. Invest in major relationships

When it comes to your physical, cognitive, emotional, social, and spiritual wellbeing, don't underestimate the importance of your family and friends. Whether it's your partner, children, close friends, colleagues, or neighbors, the people you turn to for support can play a critical role in your wellbeing.

> "If your compassion does not include yourself, it is incomplete."
>
> Jack Kornfield

Connected relationships with your family and friends can motivate you to take care of yourself—to eat right, exercise, and get regular medical care. And your family and friends can be an important buffer from the stresses of everyday life. Yet, like a garden, family and friend relationships must be tended. You can't expect to get much, if anything, out of these relationships if you're too busy or unwilling to spend quality time with people.

Slowing down and embracing the importance of spending time with family and friends will allow you to experience intimacy, play, compassion, respect, kindness, joy, and gratitude. If you're able to be truly present to your family and friends—without agendas, expectations, or preoccupations—you will feel more connected to one another by love.

EXPRESS YOURSELF:
Go to *The Understanding Your Grief Journal* on pp. 138-139.

NURTURING YOURSELF COGNITIVELY

Your mind gives you the intellectual capacity to think, absorb information, make decisions, and reason logically. Without a doubt, this capacity has also been temporarily affected by your grief. Just as your body and emotions are letting you know you've been torn apart by this loss, your mind has also, in effect, been torn apart.

Thinking normally after the death of someone precious to you would be very unlikely. Don't be surprised if you struggle with short-term memory problems, are finding it hard to focus or concentrate, have trouble making even simple decisions, or think you may be going crazy. Essentially, your mind is in a state of shock, disorientation, and confusion.

Early in your grief, you may find it helpful to allow yourself to suspend all thought and purposefulness for a time. Allow yourself

PRACTICING MINDFULNESS

There's no better way to nurture yourself cognitively than to practice mindfulness. Mindfulness is the habit of being fully present in each moment and not allowing yourself to be distracted by anything that's not here and now.

Mindfulness eases your cognitive burden because you're only thinking about one thing at a time—whatever you're doing at the moment. Forget multitasking and try uni-tasking.

But mindfulness is also a tool for soothing and deepening yourself physically, emotionally, socially, and spiritually.

When you can simply "be" in each moment, you can enjoy all the simple pleasures and daily miracles as they unfold. You can better appreciate your precious minutes here on earth. Your body relaxes. Your emotions become more serene. You grow more peacefully present to those around you. And you better connect with your divine spark and your sense of meaning and purpose.

just to be. Your mind needs time to catch up with and process your new reality. In the meantime, don't expect too much of your cognitive powers.

In the Introduction, I discussed the importance of setting your intention to journey boldly through grief and heal. Your cognitive powers are quite remarkable. Willing yourself to think something can in fact help make it come to be. As you move forward in your grief journey, your restored cognitive capacities will allow you to think about your desired reality and help make it happen.

> *"Self-care is not self-indulgence, it is self-preservation."*
>
> Audre Lord

Much of the natural experience of grief lives in the past and the imagined future. As we've discussed, it's critically important to remember the past as well as explore questions, fears, and hopes about the future. But when you're not intentionally dosing yourself with mourning in these ways, you can work on being mindfully present in the now. Mindfulness gets you out of your head and into your heart. It encourages you to be with your right-now feelings, practice self-care, and turn your awareness to your life *as you are living it.*

Mindfulness is a skill that can be learned and practiced. The more you work at it, the better you get. Not only will practicing

DIVINE SPARK

Your divine spark is the still, small voice inside you that knows your meaning and purpose. It is your spiritual core. It is the glow of your soul within you. It is your deepest, truest self.

Your divine spark has been naturally impacted by grief. You relight it by mourning authentically. You strengthen it by nurturing your spirit and feeding it with wonder, joy, gratitude, congruence, meaning, and love.

mindfulness help counterbalance your grief, it can help you find your
way back to the fullness of life again.

IDEAS FOR COGNITIVE SELF-CARE
Following are just a few ideas to get you thinking about what helps
you feel cognitively well cared for. Whatever those things are, be sure
to build at least one or two into each day.

Ask yourself two questions: What do I want? What is wanted of me?
The answers to these questions may help you not only survive the
coming months and years but learn to love life again.

First, now that the person you love is gone, what do you want? What
do you want to do with your time? What do you *not* want to do with
your time? Where do you want to live? With whom do you want to
socialize? Whom do you want to be near? These are big questions
that may take some time for you to contemplate and answer.

Second, what is wanted of you? Who needs you? Who depends
upon you? What skills and experience can you bring to others?
What are you good at? Why were you put here on this earth?
While considering what you want is important, it alone does not a
complete life make.

On a more practical level, asking yourself these questions at the start
of each day may help you focus on the here-and-now and set your
intention one day at a time. What do I want from my life today?
What is wanted of me today? Living in the moment through daily
intention-setting will help you better cope with your grief.

Make a list of goals
While you shouldn't set a particular time and course for your
healing, it may help you to make other life goals for the coming year.
Consider writing a list of short-term goals for the next three months.
Maybe some of the goals could have to do with mourning activities
(for example, making a memory book or writing thank-you notes to
people who helped at the time of the death).

Also consider making a separate list of long-term goals for the next year. Be both realistic and compassionate with yourself as you consider what's feasible and feels good and what will only add more unneeded stress to your life. Keep in mind that because of your grief, you may continue to feel more fatigued than usual. Don't overcommit, thereby setting yourself up for failure. And try to include at least one or two just-for-fun goals in this list. For example, you might want to take a class or get started on a small, enjoyable project.

> *"Almost everything*
> *will work again*
> *if you unplug it*
> *for a few minutes,*
> *including you."*
>
> Anne Lamott

If at all possible, avoid making any major changes in your life for at least two years
While it can be helpful to have goals to help you look to a brighter future, it's a mistake to march too boldly ahead. Sometimes, in an effort to obliterate the pain and "move on," mourners make rash decisions shortly after a death. Some move to a new home or city. Some quit their jobs. Some break ties with people in their life or take on new relationships too quickly. Typically these changes are soon regretted. They often end up compounding feelings of loss and complicating healing as well as creating staggering new headaches. You cannot run away from the pain, so don't make things worse by trying to. Instead, give yourself at least a full twenty-four months to consider any other major changes in your life.

Of course, sometimes you may be forced to make a significant change in your life soon after a death. Financial realities may force you to sell your house or relocate, for example. In these cases, know that you're doing what you must and trust that everything will work out.

Count your blessings
You may not be feeling very good about your life right now. You may feel that you're unlucky. You may feel you're destined to be unhappy or lonely. You may feel that the universe is conspiring against you. If

you've been having any of these feelings, it's OK. There is, indeed, a time for everything—including self-doubt, self-pity, and a sense of injustice. Indeed, they can be as normal a part of your grief as anger or sadness. Nonetheless, you are blessed. Your life has purpose and meaning, even without the presence of the person who died. It will just take you some time to think and feel this through for yourself and to actively mourn as you journey through the wilderness of your grief.

When you have the energy to do so, I hope you will purposefully think of all you have to be grateful for, both in your past and your

---

TUNING INTO YOUR LOVE LANGUAGE

In his landmark 1995 book *The Five Love Languages*, author Dr. Gary Chapman introduced the idea that human beings feel cared for by others in five primary ways:

1. Receiving gifts

2. Spending quality time together

3. Hearing words of affirmation

4. Being the beneficiary of acts of service

5. Experiencing physical touch

What's your preferred love language? Becoming aware of which love language makes you feel best cared for and encouraging your friends and family members to support you by using it will help you feel nurtured and understood in your grief. You can even use your own preferred love language on yourself as you care for yourself physically, cognitively, emotionally, socially, and spiritually.

EXPRESS YOURSELF:
Go to *The Understanding Your Grief Journal* on p. 140.

present. This is not to deny the hurt, for the hurt needs to take precedence right now. But when the timing is right, it will help to consider the things that make your life worth living, too.

EXPRESS YOURSELF:
Go to *The Understanding Your Grief Journal* on pp. 140-142.

NURTURING YOURSELF EMOTIONALLY

In Touchstone Four we explored a multitude of emotions that are common in grief and mourning. These symptoms signal that you have special needs right now—needs that require your own attention as well as the attention and support of others. Acknowledging and becoming familiar with the terrain of these emotions and practicing good emotional self-care can and will help you authentically mourn and heal in small doses over time.

> "I understand now that I'm not a mess but a deeply feeling person in a messy world. Now, when someone asks me why I cry so often, I say, 'For the same reason I laugh so often—because I'm paying attention.'"
>
> Glennon Doyle

The important thing to remember is that when we pay attention to our feelings, we honor them. Whenever a grief feeling arises, I encourage you to notice it and let it absorb your full attention for at least a few minutes. Remember—it's another facet of your love for the person who died, and it's there for a reason. It's trying to teach you something about the story of your loss or your needs moving forward. Name the feeling when you're ready. Ask it where it came from and what else it's connected to.

Embracing and befriending your feelings in this way acknowledges their right to be there and over time helps them soften. As they soften, they can better integrate with all the other feelings and experiences in your life. Instead of commanding all your heart and attention, they become part of the unique and precious tapestry that is your life.

IDEAS FOR EMOTIONAL SELF-CARE

In addition to mourning openly and honestly, which gives your normal and necessary grief feelings their due, I hope you will treat your wounded emotions with tender loving care. You're hurting. You're suffering. And while the suffering is a natural part of your love, it deserves self-compassion. Be kind to yourself in whatever ways help you feel soothed, comforted, and appropriately indulged. What those are will vary widely from person to person.

Following are just a few ideas to get you thinking about what helps you feel emotionally well cared for. Whatever those things are, be sure to build at least one or two into each day.

Reach out and touch

For many people, physical contact with another human being is comforting. In fact, it's one of the five love languages (see p. 143). That's because touch has bodily effects. When we are touched in comforting ways, our brains are flooded with dopamine, serotonin, and oxytocin. These feel-good hormones help regulate our mood and make us feel calmer and happier. What's more, touch stimulates the vagus nerve, which branches out throughout our entire bodies. Its role is to calm the nervous system, which in turn helps boost our immune systems and can lower our blood pressure and heart rate.

Have you hugged anyone lately? Held someone's hand? Put your arm around another human being? Hug someone you feel safe with. Kiss your children or a friend's baby. Walk arm in arm with a neighbor. If you are soothed by touch, you might also appreciate massage, reiki, or another type of touch therapy. Try a session and see how it feels for you.

Listen to the music

Listening to music can be very cathartic for mourners because it helps us access the full range of our feelings. Music can soothe the spirit and nurture the heart. All types of music can be healing—rock & roll, classical, blues, folk. Do you play an instrument or sing?

Allow yourself the time to try these activities again soon.

What music reminds you of the person who died? At first, listening to this special music may be too painful. But later you may find that playing music that reminds you of the person who died helps you befriend your grief and keep them alive in your heart.

Draw a "grief map"
The death of someone you love has probably stirred up all kinds of thoughts and feelings inside you. Sometimes, corralling all these varied thoughts and feelings in one place can make them feel more comprehensible. You could write about them, but you can also draw them out in diagram form.

Start with a blank sheet of paper. Make a large circle at the center and label it GRIEF. This circle represents all your thoughts and feelings since the death. Now draw lines radiating out of this circle and make a smaller bubble at the end of each of these lines. Label each bubble with a thought or feeling that has been part of your grief journey. For example, you might write ANGER in one of the bubbles. Next to the word "anger," jot down notes about why you have felt angry or what this feeling has been like for you. Do this for all your prominent thoughts and feelings.

Your grief map needn't look pretty or follow any certain rules. The most important thing is the *process* of creating it because it's an effective mourning activity. When you're finished, explain it to someone who cares about you.

Schedule something that gives you pleasure each and every day
Often mourners need something to look forward to, a reason to get out of bed each morning. It can be hard to anticipate the next day when you know you'll be experiencing pain and sadness. To counterbalance your normal and necessary grief, plan—in advance—to do something you enjoy each day. Reading, baking, going for a walk, shooting hoops, having lunch with a friend, gardening, playing video games—it doesn't matter what it is as long

as it gives you emotional respite and helps you feel comforted and soothed for a while.

EXPRESS YOURSELF:
Go to *The Understanding Your Grief Journal* on pp. 143-146.

NURTURING YOURSELF SOCIALLY

The death of someone you love has probably resulted in a very real sense of disconnection from the world around you. When you reach out to your family and friends, you are beginning to reconnect. By working to become and stay aware of the larger picture—one that includes all of the people in your life—you gain some perspective. You recognize you are part of a greater whole, and that recognition can empower you. You open up your heart to love again and be loved in return when you reach out to others. Your link to family, friends, and community is vital for your sense of wellbeing and belonging.

If you don't nurture the warm, kind relationships that still exist in your life, you will probably continue to feel disconnected and isolated. You may even withdraw into your own little cave in the wilderness and continue to grieve but not mourn. Isolation can then become the barrier that keeps you stuck in the wilderness and prevents your grief from softening over time. If this happens, you will begin to die while you are still alive. So allow your friends and family to nurture you. Let them in and rejoice in the connection. And if you have to be the one to reach out and strengthen connections, that's OK, too. You will find that it is worth every bit of the effort.

IDEAS FOR SOCIAL SELF-CARE
Following are just a few ideas to get you thinking about what helps you feel socially well cared for. Whatever those things are, be sure to build at least one or two into each day.

Recognize that your friendships will probably change
Mourners often tell me how surprised and hurt they feel when friends fall away after a death. "I found out who my friends really are," they say. Know that just as you are doing the best you can right

now, your friends are doing the best they can, too—even if it doesn't seem that way. They surely still care about you, but they may also be grieving a loss in their lives (or the same loss) or dealing with other struggles. And more to the point, many of them don't know how to be present to you in your pain. Because our culture doesn't "do

THE LONELINESS OF GRIEF

Grievers often tell me they feel lonely. They have been shattered, but the people and the world around them carry on as if nothing happened. This disconnect can make them feel isolated and alone. Has this happened to you?

Human beings are social creatures. While each of us is a capable, autonomous individual, we are not meant to exist for very long on our own. We're built to interact with and rely on others. We're built for empathy, connection, and love— especially when we're grieving.

If you're lonely, finding your way through it involves befriending yourself and befriending others. The best way to build bonds with others is through proximity, repetition, and quality time. When you're near someone frequently, you're more likely to develop a strong relationship with them. But another key factor here is quality time, which is time spent with another person in which you're focusing on each other, communicating well, and mutually empathizing.

If your wilderness of grief feels lonely, I urge you to reach out to others and work on building relationships based on proximity, repetition, and quality time. Just one or two close friendships may be enough. For some people, a grief support group can also play a significant role in both supporting you in grief and easing your loneliness.

You are a worthy person who needs and deserves connection. Open yourself to others, and make the extra effort. You will be glad you did.

EXPRESS YOURSELF:
Go to *The Understanding Your Grief Journal* on p. 146.

death," death and grief can be awkward. Your friends may not even be conscious of this reaction, but nonetheless, it affects their ability to support you.

The best way for you to respond in the face of faltering friendships is to be proactive and honest. Even though you're the one who's grieving, you may need to be the one to phone your friends and keep in touch. When you do talk to them, be honest. Tell them how you're really and truly feeling and that you need and appreciate their support. If you find that certain friends can't handle your grief talk, try sticking to lighter topics with them and lean more heavily on the friends who can be present to pain.

Over time, you will probably notice a natural attrition among your friends. Some may fade away and never come back. You will need to grieve these losses, though you will likely also find that other friendships deepen and new ones emerge.

By contrast, maybe you are one of the fortunate people who feel tremendous support and love from your family and friends after the death of someone loved. If so, rejoice that you have such wise and wonderful companions in your life, and when the time comes, offer them the same empathy and presence in return.

Find a grief "buddy"

Though no one else will grieve this death just like you, there are often many others who have had similar experiences. We are rarely totally alone in the wilderness of grief. Even when there is no guide, there are fellow travelers.

Consider finding a grief "buddy"—someone who is also mourning a death, someone you can talk to, someone who also needs a companion in grief right now. You might ask a grieving friend, neighbor, or colleague to join you, or you might find a grief buddy at a support group. Make a pact with your grief buddy to call each other whenever one of you needs to talk. Promise to listen to one another without judgment. Commit to spending time together. You might arrange to meet once a week for breakfast or lunch with your grief buddy.

Remember others who had a special relationship with the person who died

At times your appropriately inward focus will make you feel alone in your grief. But you're not alone. There are probably a number of people who cared about and miss the person who died. Think about others who were affected by the death: friends, neighbors, coworkers, distant relatives, caregivers. Is there someone outside of the primary circle of mourners who may be struggling with this death? Perhaps you could call them and offer your condolences. Or write and mail a brief supportive note, or send a text or email. If you aren't a writer, consider giving them a call or stopping by for a visit.

EXPRESS YOURSELF:
Go to *The Understanding Your Grief Journal* on pp. 147-148.

NURTURING YOURSELF SPIRITUALLY

When you are torn apart by grief, you may have many spiritual questions for which there are no easy answers: Is there a God? Why me? Will life ever be worth living again? This natural human tendency to search for meaning after a death (which is the fifth need of mourning!) is why, if I could, I would encourage all of us grievers to put down "nurture my spirit" at the top of our daily to-do lists.

My own personal source of spirituality anchors me, allowing me to put my life into perspective. For me, spirituality involves a sense of connection to all things in nature, God, and the world at large. In recent years I have intentionally worked on spending more mindful time in nature, being conscious of what I am grateful for, and being fully present to the people I care about when I'm in their company. These types of daily spiritual practices speak to my soul and help me attend to my divine spark.

I recognize that for some people, however, contemplating a spiritual life in the midst of the pain of grief can be difficult. But grief is first and primarily a spiritual journey through the wilderness. To attend to, embrace, and express your grief is itself a spiritual practice—even when you've lost your faith or are struggling to regain meaning and purpose.

If you're unsure of your capacity to connect with your spirituality in life-affirming ways, try simply approaching some of the moments in your day with the openness of a child. Embrace the pleasures that come from the simple sights, smells, sounds, tastes, and textures that greet your senses. Work on being present to and appreciating the now. If you can do this, you'll find yourself rediscovering the essentials within your soul and the spirit of the world around you.

Nurturing your spiritual self not only helps you mourn and heal your grief, it also, over time, invites you to reconnect with the world and the people around you. Your heart opens wider, and your life begins to take on renewed meaning and purpose. You may become filled with compassion for other people, particularly others who have come to know grief. You may find yourself becoming kinder, more gentle, and more forgiving of others as well as yourself.

IDEAS FOR SPIRITUAL SELF-CARE
Following are just a few ideas to get you thinking about what helps you feel spiritually well cared for. Whatever those things are, be sure to build at least one or two into each day.

Create and spend time in a sacred mourning space
Creating a sacred mourning space just for you may be one of the most loving ways you can help yourself heal. Yes, you need the support of other people, but nurturing yourself during difficult times can also involve going to exile for some time each day.

Whether indoors or out, find or make a place for solitude and contemplation. The word contemplate means "to create space for the divine to enter." Think of your space, perhaps a simple corner, room, or nook in your yard, as a place dedicated exclusively to the needs of the soul. Retreat to your space for a few minutes each day and attend to and honor your grief.

> "*When you recover or discover something that nourishes your soul and brings joy, care enough about yourself to make room for it in your life.*"
>
> Jean Shinoda Bolen

Start each new day with a meditation or prayer

For many mourners, waking up in the morning is the hardest part of their day. It's as if each time you awaken, you must confront anew the realization that someone you love is gone.

Starting the day off with tears and a heavy heart, day in and day out, is so draining. Yet it may be a necessary, unavoidable part of your grief journey, especially in the early weeks and months after the death.

When you emerge from the early days, however, you may begin to gain the energy to set the tone for your day by praying or meditating first thing in the morning. When you wake up, stretch before getting out of bed or picking up your phone. Feel the blood coursing through your body. Listen to the hum of your consciousness.

Repeat a simple affirmation or prayer to yourself, such as: "Today I will live and love fully. Today I will appreciate my life." You might also offer words of gratitude: "Thank you, God, for giving me this day. Help me to appreciate it, be present to it, and make it count."

Organize a tree planting

Trees represent the beauty, vibrancy, and continuity of life. A specially selected, located, and planted tree in a public place can honor the person who died and serve as a perennial memorial. You might plan a short ceremony for the tree planting. Or, you could ask another family member to help. Consider a personalized marker or sign, too.

For a more private option, plant a tree in your own yard. Consult your local nursery for an appropriate selection. Flowering trees are especially beautiful in the spring. You might also consider a variety of tree that the person who died loved or that reminds you of a place that was special to the person who died.

Visit the great outdoors
For many people it's restorative and energizing to spend time outside. Mourners often find nature's timeless beauty healing. The sound of birdsong or the awesome presence of an old tree can help put things in perspective.

Go on a nature walk. Or camping. Or canoeing. The farther away from civilization, the better. Mother Earth knows more about kicking back than all the stress-management experts on the planet— and she charges far less.

What was the favorite outdoor getaway of the person who died? It may be as awesome as a mountain peak or as simple as your own backyard. Wherever it is, go there if you can. Sit in quiet contemplation of your relationship. Offer up your thanks for the love you shared. Close your eyes and feel the person's spirit surround you.

Imagine the person who died in heaven
Do you believe in an afterlife? Do you hope that the person who died still exists in some way? Most mourners I've talked to are comforted by a belief or a hope that somehow, somewhere, their loved one lives on in health and happiness. For some, this belief is grounded in religious faith. For others it is simply a spiritual sense.

If you do believe in an afterlife, or if you're open to the possibility, you may feel like you can still have a kind of spiritual relationship with the person who died. You may still talk to them in the hopes that they can somehow hear you. You may send them unspoken messages every night when you go to bed. There is nothing wrong with continuing to communicate with the person who died—as long as your focus on this ongoing relationship doesn't prevent you from also interacting with and loving the people in your life who are still alive.

If you believe in a heaven, close your eyes and imagine what it might be like. Imagine the person who died strong and smiling. Imagine them waving to you. And imagine your reunion when, one day, you come to join them.

EXPRESS YOURSELF:
Go to *The Understanding Your Grief Journal* on pp. 149-152.

What Are You Doing to Take Good Care of Yourself Today?

Good self-care is always important, of course, but when you're in grief it's even more essential. If you're not taking extra-tender care of yourself physically, cognitively, emotionally, socially, and spiritually, you won't have the energy or resources you need to work on the six needs of mourning—which are themselves essential aspects of self-care in grief.

So whenever possible, I hope you will stop whatever you're busy with and take a moment to ask yourself, "What am I doing today to take good care of myself?" If you can devote even a few minutes of time every day to each aspect of self-care, you will be equipping yourself with the basic supplies you need for the journey.

Reach Out for Help

> *"Sometimes in life, you can fall down holes you can't climb out of by yourself. That's what friends and family are for—to help. They can't help, however, unless you let them know you're down there."*
>
> Meg Cabot

You've probably noticed that wild geese fly in formation. Let's consider their wisdom.

When geese fly in a "V" shape, the flapping of the wings of each individual goose results in an uplift for the bird that follows. The entire flock achieves seventy-one percent greater flying range than if each bird flew alone.

When the goose leading the flock gets tired, it rotates back into the formation, and another goose assumes the point position. As they fly, the geese also honk to each other by way of encouragement and community.

What's more, if any one goose has a problem while they're in flight, two additional geese will always drop out of formation and follow the wayward goose to the ground to help support and protect it. They remain with the goose with special needs until it can continue the journey.

If there is ever a time in life when we need to follow the example of the wild geese, it's when we come to grief.

When someone we love dies, we naturally grieve, but we must intentionally mourn if we are to renew our capacity to live and love well. In other words, mourning is what generates healing. As I've been emphasizing, this means we heal by expressing our grief outside of ourselves—bit by bit, day by day—in all the ways we find helpful and cathartic.

But it also means we heal by getting affirmation and empathy from other people all along the way. Remember, the sixth need of mourning is to receive help from others—now and always. Healing requires the support and understanding of those around you as you work on the other five needs of mourning. Healing requires paying heed to the instinctual wisdom of the geese.

I've said that the wilderness of your grief is *your* wilderness and that it's up to you to find your way through it. That's true. But paradoxically, you also need companionship as you journey. You need people who will walk beside you and help provide you with divine momentum. You do not need people who want to walk in front of you and lead you down the path they think is right, nor do you need people who want to walk behind you and not be present to your pain.

"Sometimes we need someone to just listen. Not to try and fix anything or offer alternatives, but to just be there... An ear that listens can be medicine for a heart that hurts."

Steve Maraboli

You've heard me urge you a number of times in this book to seek out the support of the people in your life who are naturally good helpers. A few solid shoulders to cry on and a handful of pairs of listening ears can make all the difference in the world.

I also want you to note that this chapter is entitled "Reach Out for Help" and not "Wait Around for Others to Reach Out to You." While you might be wishing your friends and family would be frequently stopping by, calling, texting, dropping off gifts, inviting you over for dinner, etc., unfortunately this may not be the case. So if you're not getting the support you need, the most self-compassionate thing you can do is to be proactive in seeking that support. Remember how we talked about setting your intention to heal and cultivating spiritual optimism? Reaching out to others is a critical part of this self-empowering approach to healing.

It's true that sharing your pain with others won't make it disappear. You have probably learned that already. However, it will, over time, make it more bearable. What's more, reaching out for help also connects you to other people and strengthens the bonds of love that make life seem worth living. Think of the connections in your life as the mat on a trampoline. The people who support you in grief both cradle you—supporting you and helping prevent you from sinking into despair—and as you heal, lift you up, creating a springboard to meaning and purpose, love and joy.

EXPRESS YOURSELF:
Go to *The Understanding Your Grief Journal* on pp. 154-155.

Where to Turn for Help

"There is strength in numbers," one saying goes. Another echoes, "United we stand, divided we fall." If you are grieving, you will indeed find strength and a sense of stability if you draw on an entire support system for help.

> *"The purpose of life is not to be happy. It is to be useful, to be honorable, to be compassionate, to have it make some difference that you have lived and lived well."*
>
> Ralph Waldo Emerson

Friends and family members can often form the core of your support system. Seek out people who encourage you to be yourself and who acknowledge your many thoughts and feelings about the death. What you need most now are caring, nonjudgmental listeners.

You may also find comfort in talking to a spiritual leader. When someone loved dies, it's natural for you to feel ambivalent about your beliefs and question the very meaning of life. If you belong to a faith tradition, you may want to make an appointment with a leader at your church, temple, mosque, or other place of worship. If your spiritual beliefs are more eclectic or secular, you might find it helpful to talk to a humanist clergyperson or seeker dedicated to spiritual growth and higher consciousness. You might even have friends who are spiritually grounded mentors. Someone who responds not with criticism but with empathy to all your feelings can be a valuable resource.

For many grieving people, support groups are one of the best helping resources. In a group of fellow travelers, you can connect with others who have had similar experiences, thoughts, and feelings. You will be allowed and gently encouraged to talk about the person who died as much and as often as you like. We'll talk more about support groups later in this chapter.

A professional grief counselor may also be a very helpful addition to your support system. In fact, a trained counselor can be something friends and family members often can't—an objective listener. A counselor's office can be that safe haven where you can let go of any feelings you're afraid to express elsewhere. What's more, a good counselor will then help you constructively channel those emotions. We'll be talking more about working with a counselor as well.

Remember, help comes in different forms for different people. The trick is to find the combination that works best for you and then make use of it.

EXPRESS YOURSELF:
Go to *The Understanding Your Grief Journal* on pp. 156-157.

The Rule of Thirds

In my own grief journeys and in the lives of the mourners I have been privileged to counsel, I have discovered that in general, you can take all the people in your life and divide them into thirds when it comes to grief support.

About a third of the people in your life will turn out to be neutral in response to your grief. While they may still be good companions for non-grief-related activities in your life, they are not equipped to be empathetic grief supporters. Or they may say, "If you need me, just let me know"—but then you won't hear from them again. They will neither help nor hinder you in your journey.

Another third of the people in your life will be harmful to you in your efforts to mourn and heal. While they are usually not setting out to intentionally harm you, they will judge you, they will shame you, they will try to take your grief away from you, and they will pull you off the path to healing. You will feel worse after you spend time in their company. Stay away from them as much as you can for now. Consciously or unconsciously, they will trip you up and cause you to stumble and fall.

But here's the good news: the final third of the people in your life will turn out to be truly empathetic helpers. They will have a desire to understand you and your unique thoughts and feelings about the death. They will demonstrate a willingness to be taught by you and a recognition that you are the expert of your experience, not them. They will be willing to bear witness to your pain and suffering without feeling the need to take it away from you. They will believe in your capacity to heal.

While you may find that the people in your life divide up into different proportions than thirds, seek out the friends and family members who fall into this last group. They will be your confidants and momentum-givers on your journey.

EXPRESS YOURSELF:
Go to *The Understanding Your Grief Journal* on p. 157.

How Others Can Help You: Three Essentials

While there are a multitude of ways that other people can help you in your grief, here are three important and fundamental helping goals. Effective helpers may help you:

1. Embrace hope

These are the people you know who help you feel hopeful. They sustain the presence of hope as you feel separated from those things that make life worth living. They have so much hope, you can often even borrow some of theirs. They can be present to you in your loss yet bring you a sense of trust in yourself that you can and will heal.

2. Encounter your loss
These are the people who understand the need for you to revisit and recount the pain of your loss. They help you tell your story and provide a safe place for you to openly mourn. Essentially, they give you an invitation to take the grief that is inside you and share it with them.

3. Feel companioned on your journey
These people serve as companions no matter what you're thinking or feeling on any given day. They know that extending true empathy means walking with you on the journey, not ahead of you or behind you. One of the meanings of the word "grieve" is "to bear a heavy burden." Those who companion you in your grief realize that as they help bear your burden of sorrow, they shoulder some of the weight, and they help you trust that something good will be borne of it.

EXPRESS YOURSELF:
Go to *The Understanding Your Grief Journal* on p. 158.

Reaching Out to a Support Group

For some people, grief support groups, where people come together and share the common bond of experience, can be invaluable in helping them heal. In these groups, each person can share their unique grief journey in a nonthreatening, safe atmosphere. Group members are usually very patient with you and your grief and understand your need for support long after the death.

For some mourners, grief support groups form the core of their support systems. If your friends and family lack the capacity to provide you with sufficient support beyond the early days of grief, a good support group can help fill the gap. It's also important to keep in mind that those closest to you may understandably grow grief-fatigued in the months to come. Even if you have exceptionally empathetic and supportive friends and family members, you will probably find that grief support group members can better sustain their focus on your grief (and you on theirs) over the longer term.

You might think of grief support groups as places where fellow journeyers gather. Each of you has a story to tell. Your dispatches from the wilderness help affirm the normalcy of each other's experiences. You also help each other build divine momentum toward healing.

EXPRESS YOURSELF:
Go to *The Understanding Your Grief Journal* on p. 158.

GETTING HELP IN A CRISIS

If your grief is ever so overwhelming that your life or the life of someone in your care is in danger, you are in crisis and should seek help immediately.

Signs of a crisis include:

- Thinking about, planning, or attempting suicide
- Failing to care for yourself (e.g., eating, bathing, dressing)
- Abusing alcohol or drugs

If any of these warning signs apply to you, reach out to one of the helping resources below without delay.

Call your primary-care provider
Call 911
Call 988 (starting in 2022)
Call the National Suicide Prevention Lifeline: 800-273-TALK (8255) or use the live online chat at suicidepreventionlifeline.org/chat
Text the National Crisis Text Line: text HOME to 741741 (U.S. and Canada)
Call your local emergency room

HOW TO FIND A GRIEF SUPPORT GROUP

To find a support group near you, call your local hospice or funeral home. They typically keep tabs on grief support groups in their service area and may run support groups out of their facilities, too. Googling "grief support groups near me" is another way to find options that may work for you.

A second option is to start an informal grief group of your own. If you have friends or acquaintances who are also grieving a loss, you might suggest meeting informally—maybe over breakfast once a month—to talk about your experiences. Be sure to invite only empathetic people you think would come together in the spirit of creating a safe, mutually supportive experience. Because this format lacks structure and formal leadership, it won't work for everyone, but it can sometimes be a good starting point.

You may also be interested in joining an online grief support group. This can be particularly effective if you're comfortable communicating online (such as on online video platforms and message boards) and/or are grieving a particular type of loss and would like to meet others who have suffered the same type of loss. Try Googling "grief support groups for (type of loss)" and see what comes up.

For those who choose to join a structured, in-person grief support group, I suggest that you look for a group whose members have all suffered a death loss (versus a mixture of loss types, such as divorce, health issues, etc.). I also believe that for your first grief support group experience, it's best to participate in a closed psychoeducational group with set starting and ending dates if at all possible. In these types of groups, a professional or trained lay facilitator provides some education about grief (typically by using a book such as this one) as well as time for open discussion and sharing. Members come together for a fixed number of sessions. Everyone starts and stops at the same time, often meeting once a week for a period of several months. People are not joining or leaving the group midstream.

This type of group gives members a strong foundation of basic grief and mourning principles that will help them embark on a healthy path through the wilderness and maintain momentum long after the group has ended. What's more, members have the chance to meet, bond, and graduate together. This creates a strong, cohesive group dynamic.

"Alone we can do so little; together we can do so much."

Helen Keller

After this closed group has ended, it's common for now-bonded members to continue to meet regularly for more informal support and possibly join up with past graduates of the same initial support group experience. This type of open-ended, less structured, ongoing group can be a wonderful source of long-term support, but, in general, I find that it's not the best way to get started with a grief support group.

In the beginning of your journey, you may not feel ready for a support group. It's common for shock, numbness, and other early trauma responses to make it difficult for mourners to participate in or feel helped by a support group. If this is where you find yourself, it's OK to postpone joining a group for a while and in the meantime, get individual help from a grief counselor instead. It's also OK to repeat the introductory grief group if after graduation you realize you were too psychically numb to have benefited from it.

Finally, keep in mind that grief support sources can be combined. For example, you can participate in both an in-person support group and an online support group if you wish. And you may want to see a counselor while you are participating in a support group as well. Such tandem approaches are needed for some grievers to feel adequately supported.

EXPRESS YOURSELF:
Go to *The Understanding Your Grief Journal* on p. 159.

HOW TO KNOW IF YOU'VE FOUND A HELPFUL SUPPORT GROUP
Not all support groups will be helpful to you. Sometimes the group dynamic becomes unhealthy for one reason or another. Look for the following signs of a healthy support group.

1. Group members acknowledge that each person's grief is unique. They respect and accept both what members have in common and what is unique to each person.

2. Group members understand that grief is not a disease but instead a normal process without a specific timetable or sequential steps.

3. All group members are encouraged to talk about their grief. However, if some decide to listen without sharing, their preference is respected.

4. Group members understand the difference between actively listening to what another person is saying and expressing their own thoughts and feelings. They make every effort not to interrupt when someone else is speaking.

5. Group members respect one another's right to confidentiality. Thoughts, feelings, and experiences shared in the group are not made public or shared with anyone else outside the group.

6. Each group member is allowed equal time to speak; one or two people do not monopolize the group's time.

7. Group members don't give advice to each other unless it's asked for.

8. Group members recognize that thoughts and feelings are neither right nor wrong. They listen with empathy to the thoughts and feelings of others without trying to change them.

EXPRESS YOURSELF:
Go to *The Understanding Your Grief Journal* on pp. 159-160.

Reaching Out to a Grief Counselor

I believe that individual counseling is an excellent addition to any griever's self-care plan. While it may be more necessary in cases of complicated grief, which we'll talk about next (see p. 169), even grievers encountering normal grief can benefit from the companionship of a skilled, compassionate therapist.

In the Introduction, I covered the concept of "companioning," which is the grief-counseling philosophy I advocate and teach to other grief caregivers. A good grief companion will help you feel seen, heard, affirmed, and understood. What's more, they will normalize your grief; if you're feeling like you're going crazy or doing grief "wrong," they'll assure you that what you're experiencing is normal—and if it turns out that your experience is complicated, they'll help you sort that out, too.

Grief counseling is simply a form of self-care. I've noticed that some people think of self-care wellness practices such as yoga, massage, and acupuncture as normal parts of routine physical, emotional, and spiritual maintenance, while other people construe them as overly indulgent or superfluous. When it comes to grief counseling (and all forms of self-care, really), I encourage you to align yourself with the first group. This is your one, precious life. You need and deserve holistic care, and that includes skilled grief care when you are in deep grief.

Companioning grieving people has been one of the greatest privileges of my life. If you have the resources and access, I hope you'll consider reaching out to a grief counselor as part of your sixth need of mourning. The relationship you build and the work you do in the safe place that is their meeting space can help you mourn and heal more effectively and build more meaning, purpose, and joy into your remaining days.

EXPRESS YOURSELF:
Go to *The Understanding Your Grief Journal* on pp. 160-161.

MOURNING CARRIED GRIEF

If you've suffered past losses in your life, it's common for those griefs to come up again when a new loss occurs. And as you're working your way through this book—learning about the necessity of active mourning and reaching out to others—you may also realize that, often through no fault of your own but in unknowing collusion with the people and culture around you—you've never fully and openly mourned some of those past losses.

"There is no greater agony than bearing an untold story inside you."

Maya Angelou

When this happens, it means you're probably carrying old, unreconciled grief.

Carried grief is dangerous because it's a common, invisible, insidious cause of long-term wellness issues that negatively affect your quality of life.

In my work with grieving people, I have many times found it to be at the root of struggles with anxiety, depression, pessimism, substance abuse, intimacy, and more. It mutes your divine spark, and it causes some people to die while they are alive.

If you think you may be carrying old grief, I urge you to work with a grief counselor to explore and mourn it. Each loss really needs its own consideration, and a good counselor can help you not only sort out all your intermingled griefs but also create a mourning plan to give each one some dedicated attention. Of course, the counselor will also help you actively and effectively engage with your current grief, as well.

The good news is that engaging with and reconciling longstanding carried grief can be a transformative process. I've heard mourners describe it as "waking up" and "truly living for the first time." Just imagine what might be waiting for you on the other side.

EXPRESS YOURSELF:
Go to *The Understanding Your Grief Journal* on p. 161.

HOW TO FIND A GOOD COUNSELOR

Finding a good counselor to help you through the grief process sometimes takes a little doing. A recommendation from someone you trust is probably the best place to start. If they had a good counseling experience and think you would work well with this counselor, then you might want to start there. Ultimately, though, only you will be able to determine if a particular counselor is right for you.

If a friend's recommendation doesn't work out, try contacting:

- A local hospice, which may even have a counselor on staff who may be available to work with you.

- Local grief support groups, which often maintain a list of counselors specializing in grief therapy.

- Your primary-care provider, who may be able to refer you to a bereavement-care specialist.

- A local information and referral service, such as a crisis intervention center, which may maintain a list of counselors who focus on grief work.

- A local hospital, family service agency, funeral home, and/or mental health clinic. All usually maintain a list of referral sources.

During your first counseling session, consider asking:

- Have you had specialized bereavement-care training?

- What is your experience working with grieving people?

- What is your counseling approach with a grieving person?

Trust your instincts. You may leave your first counseling session feeling you've clicked with the counselor, or it may well take you several sessions to form an opinion. Ultimately, if you feel like a counselor isn't a good fit—for whatever reason—try a different one. It's OK to have an initial consultation with a few counselors before you settle on one.

EXPRESS YOURSELF:
Go to *The Understanding Your Grief Journal* on p. 162.

LENGTH OF COUNSELING
Some grieving people only need a few sessions, while others benefit from a longer-term counseling relationship. Discuss this issue openly with your counselor and decide what's best for you.

One helpful way to determine an appropriate length of counseling is called a "time contract." With this method, the counselor and grieving person meet for an initial consultation and agree on a certain number of sessions. That number may vary considerably depending on your unique circumstances. At the end of the preestablished number of sessions, the counselor and griever decide if more sessions would be helpful. If the time contract idea appeals to you, bring it up with your counselor.

Regardless of the length of your counseling, it's doubtful you'll feel you are easily, steadily moving forward in your grief journey. More likely, the natural ebb and flow of pain and healing will at times make you feel you aren't making steady progress. This is normal. Be patient with yourself as you continue to work on the six needs of mourning.

EXPRESS YOURSELF:
Go to *The Understanding Your Grief Journal* on p. 163.

Reaching Out When Your Grief is Complicated

In some ways, all grief is complicated. Just as love is always complex and multifaceted, so too is grief. But grief counselors sometimes use the term "complicated grief" to talk about a grief experience that is *extra* complicated. It's a matter of degree, features, impact on the ability to function in daily life, and sometimes duration.

Complicated grief isn't abnormal or pathological. It's simply normal, necessary grief that has gotten amplified, stuck, or off track somehow. It has encountered barriers or detours of one kind or another and as a result has become stalled, waylaid, or denied altogether.

You might be at risk for complicated grief depending on:

The circumstances of the death
Your grief might naturally be complicated if the person you love died suddenly or unexpectedly, if a younger person died, or if the death was violent, self-inflicted, or ambiguous (such as an uncertain cause of death or an unrecoverable or missing body).

> "Loving ourselves through the process of owning our story is the bravest thing we will ever do."
>
> Brené Brown

Your personality and mental health
If you are carrying unreconciled grief from previous life losses, or if you have a tendency toward depression, you may be more susceptible to a complicated grief experience. Difficulties in expressing and managing feelings of sadness and anger, extreme dependency on the approval of others, or a tendency to assume too much responsibility may also complicate your grief journey.

Your relationship with the person who died
An intensely close relationship to the person who died can trigger complicated grief, as can ambivalent relationships and relationships marked by dysfunction, abuse, mental health issues, and separation.

Your capacity to express your grief
If you've been unable to accept the intense emotions evoked by the death, you may experience complicated grief. Or perhaps your family and friends have failed to affirm your feelings of loss. Other significant losses occurring at the same time or the inability to participate in the grief process due to illness or the lack of access to social rituals, such as a funeral, can also give rise to complicated grief.

Your use of drugs or alcohol
Drugs or alcohol overuse may suppress your feelings connected with the loss, thus short-circuiting what might otherwise be a normal and healthy grief journey.

Essentially, anything "extra" about a death or other concurrent circumstances in your life heightens the chances of complicated grief. In this book we've talked about grief overload (p. 60), traumatic loss (p. 55), anticipatory grief (p. 52), soulmate grief (p. 51), carried grief (p. 167) and other "whys" that shape your unique grief journey (Touchstone Three). The more extreme and numerous these complicating factors are for you, the more likely you are to naturally find yourself struggling. Everyone's grief wilderness is different. If yours is unusually rugged and harrowing, it's perfectly understandable that you would require additional support.

EXPRESS YOURSELF:
Go to *The Understanding Your Grief Journal* on p. 164.

CATEGORIES OF COMPLICATED GRIEF

Now and then I talk about complicated grief categories because naming them in this way can sometimes help grievers recognize their own stuck or off-track patterns of grief thoughts, feelings, and behaviors.

Unembarked grief

Unembarked grief is grief that has never been allowed to depart from the trailhead and enter the normal and necessary wilderness of grief. In other words, it is uninitiated or unlaunched grief. Carried grief is a form of unembarked grief. If you feel stuck in shock, numbness, denial, or postponing grief, you may be experiencing unembarked grief.

Impasse grief

Imagine you're hiking through the wilderness and while you're on the trail, you come up against a sheer rock face or a massive downed tree. When you encounter such an obstruction, in order to proceed you must find a way through or around it, right? Instead, people experiencing impasse grief remain stuck in that particular location. They keep butting up against the same problem. In my counseling experience, the obstruction often comes in the form of a

> *"The privilege of a lifetime is being who you are."*
>
> Joseph Campbell

pronounced and prolonged encounter with anger, anxiety, sadness, or guilt that does not soften with time and active mourning.

Off-trail grief

Sometimes grievers, usually unknowingly, take an unhelpful path. After all, it's not like there's a sign with two arrows, one saying, "Healthy grief this way" and the other, "Caution! Wrong way!" So they embark on or stumble onto a course that occupies them with other tasks and issues in lieu of their normal and necessary grief work. Off-trail grief behaviors are essentially avoidance patterns—habits and obsessions that replace the work of grief and mourning, such as:

- Displacing grief feelings onto another life issue, such as work or relationship issues

- Replacing the relationship prematurely

- Focusing on physical symptoms and problems to the exclusion of anything else

- Getting caught up in addictive behaviors, such as overworking, compulsive shopping, overeating, abusing substances, gambling, overexercising, video game playing, and more. Essentially, any consuming behavior that thoroughly distracts from the necessary work of grief and mourning.

- Traveling, often to stay on the move in the hopes of outrunning grief

- Crusading, or over-dedication to or premature involvement with a cause, often related to the circumstances of the death or the passions of the person who died

Keep in mind that in grief, many of these behaviors can be healthy in moderation and when accompanied by active mourning. If you're exercising a bit more than normal as a means of stress management, for example, that's OK as long as you're also actively encountering your grief and working on the six needs of mourning. It's a question of balance. If you're turning to these behaviors in lieu of attending to your grief and mourning, on the other hand, that's off-trail grief, and you may benefit from getting some help from a grief counselor to get back on track.

Encamped grief
Sometimes on the journey through grief, people stop moving—forward, backward, or sideways—and instead step off the trail and set up permanent residence in the wilderness. They build themselves a shelter, unpack provisions, and settle in. These grievers often begin to identify with their loss experience so strongly that they build their new self-identities around the death or the circumstances of the loss. They "become" their loss story, and it's not uncommon for them to express a sense of pride, loyalty, or honor in their encampment.

If you recognize yourself in any of these complicated grief categories, I don't want you to be alarmed or feel ashamed. They happen all the time, and they're largely products of our mourning-avoidant culture's complicity when it comes to an unhealthy understanding of grief. Instead, I hope you will feel proud of your new insight and motivated to take action to get the extra support you need and deserve.

EXPRESS YOURSELF:
Go to *The Understanding Your Grief Journal* on p. 165.

Getting Help for Complicated Grief

If you feel like you're experiencing complicated or traumatic grief, you simply need some extra help encountering the six needs of mourning. I recommend you see a grief therapist for a few sessions then take it from there. Depending on the severity of your symptoms and the degree of difficulty you're having functioning in your daily life, a few sessions may be enough to help you through the most challenging features of the terrain of your wilderness. Or you may need ongoing support for a longer period of time.

Grief counselors can range from therapists to clergy, hospice caregivers, funeral home aftercare staff, and lay-trained caregivers. Grief therapists, on the other hand, have specific clinical training, experience, and interest in grief therapy. For people challenged by complicated grief, I recommend looking for a grief therapist. Your needs will be better met by someone with more in-depth knowledge and experience.

"We've got to live, no matter how many skies have fallen."

D.H. Lawrence

Perhaps it would help to return to the concept of emotional intensive care here. While your primary-care provider's clinic is staffed by highly competent nurses and doctors, it is not the same as an intensive care unit staffed by specially trained acute-care nurses and specialists. Similarly, the appropriate level of care for normal grief is different than the appropriate level of care for complicated grief, although there is certainly a wide gray area in between.

If you're experiencing complicated grief, you have special needs, and so you need specialized care. It's as simple as that. Again, if you need help finding a grief therapist, try the same tips for finding a good counselor, on page 166—only this time ask for referrals to therapists who have experience with or specialize in caring for people challenged by complicated or traumatic grief.

EXPRESS YOURSELF:
Go to *The Understanding Your Grief Journal* on p. 166.

A Few Last Thoughts about Reaching Out for Help

As a professional grief companion, I have been privileged to have thousands of grieving people reach out to me for help. Among other important lessons, they've taught me that sharing their grief with others and receiving empathy in return are integral parts of the healing process.

I hope this touchstone has helped you understand the importance of reaching out for help in your grief. Please don't try to confront your grief alone. You need companions—friends, relatives, neighbors, community members, counselors, others who have experienced a similar loss—who will walk beside you and be your steady companions as you make the difficult journey through the wilderness of your grief.

Seek Reconciliation, Not Resolution

How do you ever find your way out of the wilderness of your grief? You don't have to wander there forever, do you?

The good news is that no, you don't have to dwell in deep grief forever. If you follow the trail markers on your journey through the wilderness, if you keep close to the touchstones, you will indeed find your way out.

> *"Loss has transformed the way I now see, breathe, and feel life. I'll never be the same person again."*
>
> Jennifer Ross

A number of psychological grief models talk about "resolution," "recovery," "reestablishment," or "reorganization" as the desired destination of your grief journey. So you might have heard—and may even believe—that your grief journey will end when you resolve, or recover from, your grief.

But you may also be coming to understand one of the fundamental truths of grief: Your journey will never truly end. People do not "get over" grief. My personal and professional experience has taught me that a total return to "normalcy" after the death of someone loved is not possible because we are all forever changed by loss. Just as with any significant experience in your life, your journey through the wilderness of grief will become a part of who you are and always live inside you.

"Reconciliation" is the term I find most appropriate for the healing that develops as you work to integrate the loss. We as human beings don't resolve or recover from our grief but instead become reconciled to it.

With reconciliation comes full acknowledgment of the reality of the death. Beyond a cognitive working through of the death, there is also an emotional and spiritual accommodation. What had been understood at the head level is now understood at the heart level. Energy and confidence are renewed, and the desire to become reinvolved in the activities of living is reawakened. There is also a deepening wisdom about the fact that pain and grief are difficult, yet necessary, parts of life.

As reconciliation unfolds over time, you will recognize that life is and will continue to be different without the person who died. Changing your relationship with them from one of presence to one of memory and redirecting your energy and initiative toward the future often take longer—and involve more hard work—than most people comprehend before they themselves suffer such a loss.

But keep in mind that reconciliation doesn't just happen. It's an active, intentional process. You reach it through deliberate mourning, by:

• talking it out.

• crying it out.

• writing it out.

• thinking it out.

• playing it out.

• painting (or sculpting, etc.) it out.

• dancing it out.

• etcetera!

YOUR PATCHWORK HEART

Your heart has been broken, maybe even torn into a million pieces. Active, intentional mourning is the process of stitching it back together.

As you approach reconciliation, your heart will become whole again. But it will be a patchwork heart. The seams where it's been sewn together will always be apparent to you, and they will twinge and ache sometimes. The wounds will be healed, yet the scars will always remain.

But still, in reconciliation you will be able to live wholeheartedly again, because your torn-apart heart will be mended.

To journey toward reconciliation requires that you descend before you can transcend. You don't get to go around or above your grief. You must go through it. And while you are going through it, you must also befriend and express what you are thinking and feeling if you are to truly reconcile yourself to it.

You will find that as you approach reconciliation, the sharp, ever-present pain of grief will give rise to a renewed sense of meaning and purpose. Your feelings of loss will never completely disappear, yet they will soften, and the intense pangs of grief will become less frequent. Hope for your continued living will grow as you are able to make commitments to the future, realizing that the person you have given love to and received love from will never be forgotten. The unfolding of this journey does not return you to an "old normal" but instead leads you to discover a new normal.

EXPRESS YOURSELF:
Go to *The Understanding Your Grief Journal* on pp. 168-169.

Signs of Reconciliation

To help you discern where you are in your movement toward reconciliation at any given time, the following list of signs of healing may be helpful. You don't have to be experiencing all of them for reconciliation to be taking place, however. In fact, if you're early in the work of mourning, you may not yet be noticing any of them yet. Be patient and remember that reconciliation is an ongoing, incremental process.

Still, this list may give you a way to keep an eye on your movement through grief. As new reconciliation signs arise, you may even want to place checkmarks next to them. The closer you get to emerging from the wilderness, the more of these signs you will probably notice.

◯ A recognition of the reality and finality of the death

◯ A return to stable eating and sleeping patterns

○ A sense of release from the person who died. You will have thoughts about the person, but you will not be preoccupied by these thoughts.

○ The enjoyment of experiences in life that are normally enjoyable

○ The establishment of new and healthy relationships

○ The capacity to live a full life without feelings of guilt or lack of self-respect

○ The drive to organize and plan your life toward the future

○ The serenity to be comfortable with the way things are rather than attempting to make things as they were

○ The versatility to welcome more change into your life

○ The awareness that you have allowed yourself to authentically, fully grieve and mourn—and you have survived

○ The understanding that you do not "get over" your grief but instead learn to live with the new reality

○ The acquaintance with new parts of yourself that you have discovered in your grief journey

○ The adjustment to new role changes that have resulted from the loss of the relationship

○ The acknowledgment that the pain of loss is intrinsic to the privilege of giving and receiving love

○ A sense of renewed meaning and purpose

Reconciliation emerges much in the way grass grows. We don't typically check our lawns each day to see if the grass is growing, but it does grow, and soon we come to realize it's time to mow the grass again. Likewise, we can't expect to examine our grief movement on a daily or weekly basis to be assured that we're healing. As we've discussed, grief, in the short term, is more of a back-and-forth, round-and-around process. Nonetheless, as long as we're consistently doing the work of mourning, we do eventually realize that over the course of months and years, we've come a long way.

Usually there is not one great moment of "arrival" but instead a series of subtle changes and incremental progress. Along the way, I hope you will stop and take the time to notice and be grateful for even very small advancements. If you're beginning to taste your food again, be thankful. If you mustered the energy to meet a friend for lunch, be grateful. If you finally got a good night's sleep, rejoice.

Here's what C. S. Lewis wrote in *A Grief Observed* about his grief symptoms as they eased in his journey to reconciliation:

"There was no sudden, striking, and emotional transition. Like the warming of a room or the coming of daylight, when you first notice them, they have already been going on for some time."

Of course, the journey toward reconciliation is not an expressway to healing. Even when you're feeling good divine momentum, you're likely to take some steps backward from time to time. That's to be expected. When it happens, be kind to yourself and keep believing in yourself. Set your intention to continue to reconcile your grief, and foster hope that you can and will come to live and love fully again.

EXPRESS YOURSELF:
Go to *The Understanding Your Grief Journal* on pp. 169-170.

Managing Your Expectations

Movement toward reconciliation in grief is often draining and exhausting. It also can take a very long time. Many grieving people have unrealistic expectations about how readily they should be feeling forward momentum, and when it takes much longer and involves a lot more hard work than they ever imagined, they sometimes experience a loss of self-confidence and self-esteem. They begin to question their capacity to heal. They doubt things will ever get better. They lose hope. If you find yourself in this situation, you're not alone.

If you're feeling doubtful or hopeless, consider if you've consciously or unconsciously set a timetable for reconciliation. Ask yourself questions like, "Have I mistakenly given myself a deadline for when I should be 'over' my grief? Am I expecting myself to heal more quickly than is possible?" If the answer to such questions is yes, recognize that you could be hindering your own healing by expecting too much of yourself too soon. In fact, accepting the pace of your unique journey through your singular wilderness is key to eventual reconciliation. Take your grief and your healing as they come, one day at a time.

"Everything is gestation and then bringing forth."

Rainer Maria Rilke

One valuable way to make the most of the day-by-day nature of mourning work is to use the companion journal to this book. Write out your many thoughts and feelings, and you will be amazed at how it helps you embrace your grief. But in addition, your journal then becomes a written record of your experience. You can pick it up at any time and reacquaint yourself with your earlier thoughts and feelings. This can help you see the many changes that will have unfolded as you've engaged with the six needs of mourning over the course of your grief journey.

You can't control death or ignore your human need to grieve and mourn when it impacts your life. You do have the choice, however, to help yourself heal. Embracing and expressing your grief is probably some of the hardest work you will ever do. As you do this work, surround yourself with compassionate, loving people who are willing to walk with you, and try to be unfailingly kind to yourself.

EXPRESS YOURSELF:
Go to *The Understanding Your Grief Journal* on pp. 170-171.

Not Attached to Outcome

I understand that managing expectations for healing in grief can be difficult. When we're struggling and in pain, it's natural to want to feel better as soon as possible.

Yet reconciling deep grief is not a fast or efficient process. So if we can let go of any expectations for healing quickly or in a certain way, we actually end up suffering less. The practices of accepting what is in each moment and mindfully living in the now as much as possible are what allow us to be present to our grief and our life—which in turn speeds healing and enhances our quality of life.

The Zen concept of nonattachment to outcome applies here. When we take meaningful action without worrying too much about the outcome of that action, we're doing what we can and beyond that, surrendering the illusion of control. Yes, we still can and should intentionally mourn, connect with others, take good care of ourselves, foster hope, and envision our meaningful futures (all activities we *can* control). But that's where we let go. **In short, we act with intention, then what happens, happens.**

That's exactly how the magic of mourning works. If you take meaningful action to work a bit on one or more of the six needs of mourning most days, you don't need to worry about the outcome of those actions. You can simply trust that over time the mourning will generate divine momentum to carry you toward healing, even if there are lots of ups and downs along the way.

> "You will lose someone you can't live without, and your heart will be badly broken, and the bad news is that you never completely get over the loss of your beloved. But this is also the good news. They live forever in your broken heart that doesn't seal back up. And you come through. It's like having a broken leg that never heals perfectly, that still hurts when the weather gets cold, but you learn to dance with the limp."
>
> Anne Lamott

Whenever I have a counseling appointment to see someone who's grieving, right before they're due to arrive, I spend a few minutes in silence repeating this three-phase mantra to myself:

No rewards for speed.

Not attached to outcome.

Divine momentum.

As you undertake the long, arduous journey toward reconciliation of grief, this same affirmation can support you, too.

EXPRESS YOURSELF:
Go to *The Understanding Your Grief Journal* on p. 172.

Choosing Hope for Your Healing

In addition to grief work, permitting yourself to have hope is central to achieving reconciliation. As we've said, hope is trust in a good that is yet to be.

I think about a man I was honored to companion following the tragic death of his seven-year-old son, Adam, in a car accident. This father was heartbroken. His divine spark was all but snuffed out. He had come to know the deepest despair. Yet in our time together, he discovered that if he were ever to truly live again, he would have to work *through* his grief. So, he adopted the mantra, "Work on!"

Refusing to give in to despair may be the greatest act of hope there is. In his process of conscious intention-setting, he decided to believe that even the most agonizing loss can be survived. Yes, like him, you have gone to the wilderness. Darkness may seem to surround you. But also rising up within you is the profound awareness that the pain of your grief is an inextricable part of the love you shared with the person who died. Your love is still there. You are still here. **You have an unknown number of precious days left on this earth to honor that love and find ways to love others—and yourself—even better.**

And so you choose to hope and to work on. Living in the present moment of your pain while having hope for a good that is yet to be are not mutually exclusive. They are the yin and yang of the grief journey. Like grief and love, they coexist, each deepening the experience of the other.

> *"You don't heal from the loss of a loved one because time passes. You heal because of what you do with the time."*
>
> Carol Crandell

EXPRESS YOURSELF:
Go to *The Understanding Your Grief Journal* on p. 173.

Borrowing Hope

But what if you don't feel hopeful? What if you're having a hard time mustering hope? This can happen in grief, and when it does, it's perfectly understandable. Sinking into hopelessness does not mean you're weak or incapable. If you're not suffering from concurrent clinical depression, it simply means your grief may have dipped into a difficult low or may be more complicated—and you need extra support.

If you're struggling with maintaining hope, you can reach out to a support group or a grief counselor, as we discussed in the last chapter. Those are always good avenues. But you can also borrow hope.

I bet you know people who exude hope. Some are empathetic listeners, and simply talking to them about your grief can help ease your sense of hopelessness. Others are survivors of a similar loss, and their wisdom about how it gets better can rekindle your hope. And still others just seem to have hope to spare. They tend to be happy, joyful people. Spending time with them can lift your spirits.

On your journey to reconciliation, remember that you can borrow hope if you're ever feeling stalled or stuck. It's a good practice for regaining momentum.

EXPRESS YOURSELF:
Go to *The Understanding Your Grief Journal* on p. 173.

The Safety Net of Faith

Sometimes in my own journeys through the wilderness of grief, when hope has seemed absent, I have found that faith could sustain me. To me faith can feel like a safety net beneath hope. When hope fails, faith is there to catch me.

You've heard the phrase "blind faith." Actually, that's redundant because all faith is blind. Having faith means believing and trusting in something that has no logical proof or material evidence. I think that the alternative—believing in only what we can see and experience with our five physical senses—is unnecessarily limiting and can deaden our hope and sense of wonder.

On your journey to reconciliation, faith is a bridge that can help you get from your now to your future. Right now your bridge might feel like a wobbly wooden pathway swinging over a great chasm, or it might seem as sturdy and transcendent as the Golden Gate—or somewhere in between. Regardless, to walk your bridge you must put one foot in front of the other, trusting that it will support you.

My own faith is inspired by moments when I'm able to notice the good, sweet, and tender in life, despite the deep wounds of my grief. Stories of the indomitable human spirit give me faith. Opening my heart to the mysteries of spirituality and the universe gives me faith. Your faith may be anchored in religious beliefs or other concepts and experiences. But regardless of the source and nature of your faith, if you lose hope along your journey, I invite you to join me in falling back on faith.

EXPRESS YOURSELF:
Go to *The Understanding Your Grief Journal* on p. 174.

You Will Get There

For many of you just starting out or in the thick of your journey through the wilderness of grief, reconciliation may seem like an impossibly distant destination. It's true that it usually takes a long time and a lot of hard work to get there. But I promise you it's there, waiting for you.

Every day that you authentically encounter and engage with your grief, you're getting one step closer—even if feels like you're going backward. Each moment you actively work on one of the six needs of mourning, you're getting one step closer. Every time you reach out for help or openly and honestly express your grief, you're getting one step closer.

> "To believe in something not yet proved and to underwrite it with our lives—it is the only way we can leave the future open."
>
> Lillian Smith

As long as you're doing the hard work of mourning, you'll find meaning and purpose, and your grief will become a part of you. As Anne Lamott says in the quote on page 184, "You will learn to dance with the limp."

Appreciate Your Transformation

The journey through grief is life-changing. When you leave the wilderness of your grief, you are simply not the same person you were when you entered it. You have been through so much. How could you be the same?

Especially if you've made it through the early days and are a few months or more into your grief journey, I imagine you are discovering that you are being transformed by the experience. Transformation literally means an entire change in form. Many mourners have said to me some variation on, "I have grown from this experience. I'm a different person." You are indeed different now. Your inner form is changing. You are likely growing in your wisdom, understanding, and compassion.

> *"The most beautiful people we have known are those who have known defeat, known suffering, known struggle, known loss, and have found their way out of the depths. These persons have an appreciation, a sensitivity, and an understanding of life that fills them with compassion, gentleness, and a deep loving concern. Beautiful people do not just happen."*
>
> Dr. Elisabeth Kübler-Ross

Don't get me wrong. Believe me, I understand that any growth you may be experiencing resulted from something you would have preferred to avoid. Though grief can indeed transform into growth, none of us would seek out the pain of loss in an effort to experience this growth. While I have come to believe that our greatest gifts often do come from our wounds, these are not wounds we masochistically go looking for. I often call it **"enforced life learning."**

When others offer untimely comments like, "You'll grow from this," your right to be hurt, angry, or deeply sad is taken away from you. It's as if these people are saying that you should be grateful for the death! Of course you're not grateful for the death (though you may feel relieved if the death followed a long period of suffering). You would rather the person you love were still alive and well—and you would probably trade all the growth in the world for just five more minutes with them.

Of course, this isn't possible. You are grieving, and I sincerely hope you are authentically mourning.

To understand how transformation in grief occurs, let's explore some aspects of growth in grief.

"I know now that we never get over great losses; we absorb them, and they carve us into different, often kinder, creatures."

Gail Caldwell

EXPRESS YOURSELF:
Go to *The Understanding Your Grief Journal* on p. 176.

Change Is Growth

We as human beings are forever changed by the death of someone important to us. You may discover that you are developing new attitudes. You may be becoming more patient or more sensitive to the feelings and circumstances of others, especially those suffering from loss. You may be becoming less patient with things that don't really matter. You may be developing new skills. You may be learning to fix your own technology problems or how to cook a nice meal. You may be arriving at new insights and decisions about how to live your new life.

You are new—different than you were prior to the death. To the extent that you are different, you can say you have grown. Yes, change is growth.

EXPRESS YOURSELF:
Go to *The Understanding Your Grief Journal* on p. 177.

Befriending Impermanence Is Growth

Life is like a river. We are floating down a river that twists and turns. We can never see very far ahead. We can never go back. Sometimes the going is smooth; sometimes the rapids are rocky and dangerous. And sometimes a waterfall plunges us over the edge.

> *"Life is either a daring adventure or nothing. To keep our faces toward change and behave like free spirits in the presence of fate is strength undefeatable."*
>
> Helen Keller

Life is constant change, which means the circumstances in which we love and are attached to things are also constantly changing. No matter how hard we try to manage risk and control our destinies, things inevitably happen that turn our lives upside-down.

Anytime we gain something new, we give something else up. Sometimes we choose the things or people to give up. Other times they're torn away from us against our will. Either way, we're bound to suffer loss.

Love and attachment are indeed wonderful, but the circumstances of life are impermanent. The globe spins. The years pass. And things change. Then change again.

The journey through grief is in part a reckoning with the transitory nature of life. The more you come to reconcile yourself to the constancy of change, the more conscious you become. Yes, befriending impermanence is growth.

EXPRESS YOURSELF:
Go to *The Understanding Your Grief Journal* on p. 177.

Finding a New Normal Is Growth

While your work of mourning will help you regain some sense of normalcy, it is a new normal. And as you work to figure out and accommodate the new normal, you are likely to try new things and stretch yourself in ways you didn't know you were capable of.

Grieving people sometimes remark to me that they never would have predicted their current life. As they set off to find a new normal, they got caught up in new interests and met new people.

But even for those grievers whose lives look more or less the same from the outside, there is a shift to a new normal inside. There is a new inner balance. Yes, finding a new normal is growth.

EXPRESS YOURSELF:
Go to *The Understanding Your Grief Journal* on p. 178.

Exploring Your Assumptions about Life Is Growth

The death of someone in your life invites you to look at your assumptions about life. Your loss experiences have a tendency to transform your values and priorities. What you may have thought of as being important—your nice house, your new car—may not matter any longer. The job or sport or financial goal that used to drive you may now seem trivial.

You may ask yourself, "Why did I waste my time on these things?" You may go through a reevaluation or a transformation of your previously held values. You may value material goods and status less. You may now more strongly value relationships.

When someone loved dies, you may also find yourself questioning your religious and spiritual values. You might ask questions like, "Why did God let this happen?" or "Why did this happen to our family?" or "Why should I get my feet out of bed?"

Exploring these questions is a long and arduous part of the grief journey. But ultimately, exploring your assumptions about life can make these assumptions richer and more life-affirming. Every loss in life calls out for a new search for meaning, including a natural struggle with spiritual concerns, often transforming your vision of your God and your faith life. Yes, exploring your assumptions about life is growth.

EXPRESS YOURSELF:
Go to *The Understanding Your Grief Journal* on p. 178.

Embracing Vulnerability Is Growth

Grief makes us feel vulnerable, and we tend not to like feeling vulnerable. But it turns out there is great power in vulnerability.

When we learn to embrace vulnerability in grief, we learn to be OK with expressing our deepest, truest feelings. We learn to openly share our souls with others. We learn to be genuine and authentic. And when all of this happens, miracles unfold.

> *"Vulnerability is not about fear and grief and disappointment. It is the birthplace of everything we're hungry for."*
>
> Brené Brown

Stoic strength is actually weakness. Vulnerability is what's genuine, connecting, and life-affirming. In fact, one of the miracles of vulnerability is that it opens your life not only to healing but also to more joy.

To be vulnerable is to take risks to reach for what we want in life. There is no other way to get where we want to go. And even though we sometimes make mistakes and things don't always unfold as we wish they would, the rewards of wielding vulnerability are ultimately so much greater than the deadening missed opportunities of staying closed-up and safe.

EXPRESS YOURSELF:
Go to *The Understanding Your Grief Journal* on p. 179.

Learning to Use Your Potential Is Growth

The grief journey often challenges you to reconsider the importance of using your potential. In some ways, death loss seems to free the potential within. Questions such as "Who am I? What am I meant to do with my life?" often naturally arise during grief. Answering them inspires a hunt. You may find yourself searching for your very soul.

In part, seeking purpose means living inside the question, "Am I spending my time doing what I really want to do?" Beyond that, it means asking, "Does my life really matter?" Rather than dragging you down, your grief may ultimately lift you up. Then it becomes up to you to embrace and creatively express your newfound potential.

Until you make peace with your purpose and using your potential, you may not experience contentment in your life. Joy will come to you when you know in your heart that you are using your potential—in your work or in your free time or in your relationships with friends and family.

"If we did all the things we are capable of, we would literally astound ourselves."

Thomas Edison

I believe that grief's call to use your potential is why many mourners go on to help others in grief. You don't have to discover a cure for cancer. You may volunteer to help out with a grief support group or a local hospice. You may reach out to a neighbor who is struggling or devote more time to your children or grandchildren. Remember—we all have gifts, and part of our responsibility is to discover what those gifts are and put them to use. Yes, learning to use your potential is growth.

EXPRESS YOURSELF:
Go to *The Understanding Your Grief Journal* on pp. 179-180.

Your Responsibility to Live

Paradoxically, it is in opening your broken heart that you open yourself to fully living until you die. You are on this earth for just a short time. You move through new developmental and spiritual stages daily, weekly, yearly.

Sorrow is an inseparable dimension of our human experience. We suffer after a loss because we are human and we are privileged to love. And in our suffering, we are transformed. While it hurts to suffer the loss of someone we love, the alternative is apathy. Apathy literally means the inability to suffer, and it results in a lifestyle that avoids human relationships to avoid suffering.

Perhaps you have noticed that some people die a long time before they stop breathing. They have no more promises to keep, no more people to love, no more places to go. It is as if the souls of these people have already departed. Don't let this happen to you. Choose life!

Yes, you have to do your work of mourning and discover how you are changed. **You have to live not only for yourself but also, I believe, for the precious person in your life who has died**—to work on their unfinished work and to realize their unfinished dreams. I truly believe that those who die before us live on through us, in our actions and our deeds. When we honor their unfinished contributions to the living world, our dead live on. When we dedicate ourselves to helping others who come to know grief, they live on.

"You attend the funeral. You grieve. Then you continue with your life. And at times the fact of her absence will hit you like a blow to the chest, and you will weep. But this will happen less and less as time goes on. She is dead. You are alive. So live."

Neil Gaiman

If, on the other hand, you have in any way set your intention to live in pessimism and chronic sorrow, you are not honoring your grief, you are dishonoring the life and death of the person who died.

What if the person who died could return to see what you are doing with your life? What if they are somehow watching you right now? Would they like how you have been transformed? Would they be proud of you? Would they believe that their life and death brought meaning and purpose to your life? Or would they see you dying before you are dead?

What if they could see that you have mourned but also gone on to help others in grief and sorrow? What if they could see that they left their love forever in your heart? What if they could see that you live your life with passion in testimony to them?

No matter how deep your grief or how anguished your soul, bereavement does not free you from your responsibility to live until you die. The gift of life is so precious and ephemeral. Choose life!

EXPRESS YOURSELF:
Go to *The Understanding Your Grief Journal* on pp. 180-182.

Nourishing Your Transformed Soul

Yes, your soul has been transformed by the death of someone loved. Your soul is not a physical entity; it is everything about you that is not physical—your values, your identity, your memories, even your sense of humor. Naturally, grief work impacts your soul! I often say that grief work is soul work.

In part, nourishing your grieving soul is a matter of surrendering to the mystery of grief. As I noted in the beginning of this book, real learning comes when we surrender: surrender our need to compare our grief (it's not a competition); surrender our self-critical judgments (we need to be self-compassionate); and surrender our need to completely understand (we never will). My hope is that the contents of this book have nourished your grieving soul.

There are, of course, many ways to nourish your grieving soul. Here are some that work for me. I nourish my soul...

- By attending to those things in life that give my life richness and purpose.

- By trying to fulfill my destiny, by developing my soul's potential.

- By striving to give back what others have given to me.

- By learning to listen to what is going on around and within me to help me decide which direction I need to go.

- By having gratitude for family and friends.

- By observing what is requesting my attention and giving attention to it.

- By finding passion in ministering to those in grief.

- By going out into nature and having gratitude for the beauty of the universe.

- By praying that I'm living on purpose and using my gifts, whether by writing a book, teaching a workshop, or caring for my grandchildren.

- By setting aside time to go into exile and be by myself in stillness.

- By earning my living doing something I love to do.

- By going through my own struggles and griefs and realizing that it is working through these wounds that helps unite me with others.

How do you nourish your transformed soul? What can you do today—and each and every day henceforth—to pay homage to your transformation? How do you most authentically live your transformed life? These are the questions of your present and future life. It is in honoring these questions that you appreciate your transformation and live the best life you can.

EXPRESS YOURSELF:
Go to *The Understanding Your Grief Journal* on p. 182.

Doing the Work—Today and Tomorrow

Depending on where you are in your grief journey, you may not be ready to fully engage with or feel inspired and encouraged by the contents of this touchstone. Yet even if this is the case for you, I believe it can help you hold onto hope for what can and will be if you continue to do the hard work of active, intentional, hopeful mourning.

If you're beginning to experience and embrace glimmers of the transformations we've been discussing in this touchstone, I encourage you to continue the authentic grief work you are doing.

Bearing witness to mourners' growth has been one of the greatest privileges of my career.

Either way, you are where you are today, and there is more work to be done tomorrow. The sun will rise again, and with the new day will come new opportunities.

Yes, out of the dark and into the light!

A Final Word

Thank you for stepping through this book with me. I hope it has been a helpful companion for you as you have worked to understand, embrace, and express your grief. Depending on where you are in your grief journey, I encourage you to reread it (or parts of it) from time to time. You will find that your insight changes and deepens over the course of months and years.

If you have also found journaling about your grief helpful, I urge you to keep going with that as well. If you feel like you are well on your way to reconciling your grief, you may want to move on to gratitude journaling instead.

When all is said and done, you love and you grieve. You grieve and you love.

I invite you to remember the power of "and" as you live your one precious life from here forward. It may help you choose to be present, to live with intention and action, to seek joy and transformation.

Whenever you feel stuck, whisper to yourself:

I am grieving *AND* I am present to all that is good in my life.

I feel lost *AND* I am finding my way.

I miss the person who died *AND* I choose joy.

I am bereft *AND* I am actively loving others in my life.

I grieve *AND* I love.

I love *AND* I mourn.

You have learned to watch for trail markers in your grief. Now learn to watch for trail markers in your continued living. Listen to the wisdom of your inner voice. Make choices that are congruent with what you have learned on your journey.

Right now, take a moment to close your eyes, open your heart, and remember the smile of the person who died.

I hope we meet one day.

The Mourner's Bill of Rights

You are the one who is grieving, and as such, you have certain "rights" no one should try to take away from you.

The following list is intended both to empower you to heal and to decide how others can and cannot help. This is not to discourage you from reaching out to others for help but rather to assist you in distinguishing useful responses from hurtful ones.

1. **You have the right to experience your own unique grief.**
   No one else will grieve in exactly the same way you do. So, when you turn to others for help, don't allow them to tell what you should or should not be feeling.

2. **You have the right to talk about your grief.**
   Talking about your grief will help you heal. Seek out others who will allow you to talk as much as you want, as often as you want, about your grief. If at times you don't feel like talking, you also have the right to be silent.

3. **You have the right to feel a multitude of emotions.**
   Confusion, disorientation, fear, guilt, and relief are just a few of the emotions you might feel as part of your grief journey. But others may judge you. They may try to tell you that feeling angry, for example, is wrong. Don't take these judgmental responses to heart. Instead, find listeners who will accept your feelings without condition.

4. **You have the right to be tolerant of your physical and emotional limits.**
   Your feelings of loss and sadness will probably leave you feeling fatigued. Respect what your body and mind are telling you. Get daily rest. Eat balanced meals. And don't allow others to push you into doing things you don't feel ready to do.

5. **You have the right to experience "griefbursts."**
   Sometimes, out of nowhere, a powerful surge of grief may overcome you. This can be frightening, but it is normal and natural. Find someone who understands and will let you talk it out.

6. **You have the right to make use of ritual.**
   A meaningful funeral can help you embark on a helpful path to healing. But even long after the funeral, you can still use the power of grief rituals to facilitate your mourning. You can carry out a number of small, personal rituals and larger group ceremonies over time to help reconcile your grief.

7. **You have the right to embrace your spirituality.**
   Grief is foremost a spiritual journey. You have the right to nurture your spirit and find ways to tend to your divine spark.

8. **You have the right to search for meaning.**
   You may find yourself asking, "Why did they die? Why this way? Why now?" Some of your questions may have answers, but some may not. And watch out for the clichéd responses some people may give you. Comments like, "It was God's will" or "Think of what you still have to be thankful for" are not helpful, and you do not have to accept them.

9. **You have the right to treasure your memories.**
   Memories are one of the best legacies that exist after the death of someone loved. You will always remember. Instead of ignoring your memories, actively engage with them and find others with whom you can share them.

10. **You have the right to move toward your grief and heal.**
    Reconciling your grief will not happen quickly. Remember, grief and mourning are best experienced in doses. Be patient and tolerant with yourself and avoid people who are impatient and intolerant with you. Neither you nor those around you must forget that the death of someone loved changes your life forever.

Helping Resources

In addition to local resources in your community, these national organizations are good sources of information and support.

LOSS OF A SPOUSE OR PARTNER
AARP, Widowed Persons Services
Independent branches of this organization can be found by searching online for Widowed Persons Service and the name of your town or state.
aarp.org

Modern Widows Club
844-4-A-WIDOW • modernwidowsclub.com

The National Widowers' Organization, Inc.
1-800-309-3658 • nationalwidowers.org

LOSS OF A CHILD
American Childhood Cancer Organization
855-858-2226 • acco.org

The Compassionate Friends
877-969-0010 • compassionatefriends.org

COPE Foundation
516-832-2673 • copefoundation.org

Mothers Against Drunk Driving (MADD)
877-ASK-MADD • 877-MADD-HELP • MADD.org

Parents of Murdered Children
513-721-5683 • 888-818-POMC • pomc.org

INFERTILITY, PREGNANCY, AND INFANT LOSS
American SIDS Institute
239-431-5425 • sids.org

International Council on Infertility Information Dissemination (INCIID)
646-961-3868 • inciid.org

Share
636-947-6164 • nationalshare.org

FOR GRIEVING CHILDREN
The Dougy Center
503-775-5683 • dougy.org

National Alliance for Grieving Children (U.S. and Canada)
866-432-1542 • childrengrieve.org

SUICIDE LOSS AND PREVENTION
American Association of Suicidology
202-237-2280 • 1-800-273-TALK • text HOME to 741741
suicidology.org

The Samaritans
617-536-2460 • 1-877-870-HOPE • samaritanshope.org

The TREVOR Project (for LGBTQ youth)
1-866-488-7386 • thetrevorproject.org

VICTIMS AND SURVIVORS
National Organization for Victim Assistance (NOVA)
703-535-6682 • trynova.org

Safe Horizon
212-577-7700 • 1-800-621-HOPE • safehorizon.org

Tragedy Assistance Program for Survivors (TAPS)
1-800-959-TAPS • taps.org

TERMINAL ILLNESS
American Cancer Society
1-800-227-2345 • www.cancer.org

National Hospice and Palliative Care Organization
703-837-1500 • nhpco.org

GENERAL MENTAL HEALTH
National Alliance on Mental Health (NAMI)
703-524-7600 • 1-800-950-NAMI • www.nami.org

National Institute of Mental Health Public Inquiries
1-866-615-6464 • nimh.nih.gov

Substance Abuse and Mental Health Services Administration (SAMHSA)
1-877-SAMHSA • 1-800-622-HELP • samhsa.gov

National Mental Health Consumers' Self-Help Clearinghouse
mhselfhelp.org

CANADIAN RESOURCES
Bereaved Families of Ontario
bereavedfamilies.net

Canadian Hospice Palliative Care Association
613-241-3663 • www.chpca.ca

Canadian Mental Health Association
416-646-5557 • 1-833-456-4566 • cmha.ca

Canadian Virtual Hospice
mygrief.ca

Children and Youth Grief Network
childrenandyouthgriefnetwork.com

Crisis Services Canada
1-833-456-4566 • or text 45645 • crisisservicescanada.ca

Further Reading

Dr. Wolfelt has written many books to help grieving people. In addition to the one you're holding in your hands, you may be interested in reading others—especially those focused on your unique loss or experience.

THE UNDERSTANDING YOUR GRIEF SERIES

The Understanding Your Grief Journal

365 Days of Understanding Your Grief

The Wilderness of Grief: Finding Your Way

The Wilderness of Grief Audiobook

The Understanding Your Grief Support Group Guide (for group leaders)

NIGHTSTAND BOOKS
(to read for a few minutes in the morning or before sleep)

Grief One Day at a Time

First Aid for Broken Hearts

365 Days of Understanding Your Grief

One Mindful Day at a Time

Healing Your Grieving Heart

The Journey through Grief

Loving from the Outside In, Mourning from the Inside Out

Eight Critical Questions for Mourners

The Paradoxes of Mourning

Healing a Child's Grieving Heart

Healing a Friend's Grieving Heart

Healing a Teen's Grieving Heart

The Mourner's Book of Courage

The Mourner's Book of Faith

The Mourner's Book of Hope

Index